Also from GHF Press

Making the Choice
When Typical School Doesn't Fit Your Atypical Child

Forging Paths
Beyond Traditional Schooling

If This is a Gift, Can I Send it Back?
Surviving in the Land of the Gifted and Twice Exceptional

Learning in the 21st Century
How to Connect, Collaborate, and Create

How to Work and Homeschool
Practical Advice, Tips, and Strategies from Parents

Educating Your Gifted Child
How One Public School Teacher Embraced Homeschooling

Self-Directed Learning
Documentation and Life Stories

Gifted, Bullied, Resilient:

A Brief Guide for Smart Families

By Pamela Price

Edited by Sarah J. Wilson

Published by GHF Press
A Division of Gifted Homeschoolers Forum
3701 Pacific Ave. SE - PMB #609
Olympia, WA 98501

ISBN-13: 978-0692465974 (GHF Press)
ISBN-10: 0692465979

Cover design by Shawn Keehne.
www.shawnkeehne.com • skeehne@mac.com

Dedication

This book is dedicated to my darling family, especially the young man who teaches me how to be a better human being, and to the dozens of families who have so generously shared their stories with me.

Contents

Acknowledgments

In addition to my beloved family, I owe a debt of gratitude to the enlightened, thoughtful 175+ members of my blog's private online salon. You are bright spots in my daily life, a reminder of the goodness that comes through sustained, honest human connection.

Several good friends—specifically (and off the top of my head) Jade Rivera, the Yamtichs, Jen Merrill, the Hattons, Jami Milton, Mona Chicks, Denise Moore, Paige Miller, Sarah Bowland, Susanne Thomas, Kelly Xavier, Debi Pfitzenmaier, Brenda Burmeister, Heather Martin, Tedra Osell, Eva Stern, Paula Prober, Maggie McMahon, Pam Humphrey, and my old pal Bob—provided food for thought, suggestions, recommendations, and/or their personal and professional perspectives on the topic at various stages of my research and writing.

Thank you all.

The Texas Association for the Gifted and Talented (TAGT) graciously allowed me to present twice on this book's topic during the winter of 2015. The opportunity to share what I had discovered with TAGT parents proved transformative.

Finally, I would like to thank the GHF (Gifted Homeschoolers Forum) staff, volunteer, and leadership teams, GHF Press, and the GHF Bloggers community for their commitment to our common cause: nurturing gifted families through our words, works, and deeds.

Prologue

Three Vignettes

Imagine you are a child standing on a playground behind your elementary school. It is the middle of recess on a warm spring day. You are a girl, eight or nine years of age.

While the other children scamper about and happily play on seesaws, swings, and the monkey bars, you are *alone*. Once again you are excluded by the same small group of girls, a pack that alternates between being your friends and your sworn enemies. You are unsure what you have done wrong *this time*, but they have made it clear that they do not like you.

One of them actually used those words earlier: "Hey, we don't *like* you."

They tell you that a lot. They also change the reasons why they do not like you.

Sometimes they say you talk too much.

Sometimes they say you think you are smarter than they are.

Other times they say that you dress funny or your hair is too curly and weird.

Occasionally, they decide that they do they like you. For a few days you enjoy the feeling of acceptance. Yet, it still feels awkward.

Some days you feel anger rise up and you spout off to the clique's ringleader that you do not like the way they treat you and other kids. She mocks you openly. Once you became so frustrated with the perpetual cycle of your being liked/not liked/liked/not liked that you made a diagram illustrating the aggression cycle in the clique. You shared it with the girls in hopes of resolving the problem and working collaboratively on a solution.

That encounter did not go well. They called you "weird." They rolled their eyes while pointing one finger at their temples and twisting their wrists to make loops in the air. *Crazy.*

You wept. You only wanted to help and you used your powers of observation and curiosity and your innate sense of social justice to come up with a plan. No one cared. *You're weird.*

For you, school is a drag. You get frequent stomachaches from anxiety. They hurt so much you think you might die. Your chest hurts. Your head hurts. You dread the bus ride to school and back. Decades later you will loathe the smell of burnt cinnamon rolls because it smells like the school cafeteria—where you experienced profound isolation and pain.

Most days when you get home from school, you are so worn out from the emotional gamesmanship that you overwhelm your mother by discharging words and feelings. You can tell that your frustration in turn makes her uncomfortable and angry. Together you feel powerless and overwhelmed.

***

Imagine you are a kindergarten boy. Your name is Sam. You have a lot of energy in your body, and when you were little you taught yourself to read. You do not like to write. The pencil feels uncomfortable in your hand.

Everyone said that school would be fun. Your parents gave you a book before you began kindergarten. It promised that "big kid school" would be even more fun than preschool.

It's not.

Not for you.

The work they give you to do is no fun. It's dull. When you struggle to write, your teacher says that the problem is that you are not giving your best. *You should try harder.*

Recess sounded good, but you cannot find a friend to play with. Everyone else seems to have a friend—even that mean kid from the bus, Frank.

Frank likes to make fun of your favorite Doctor Who hat. He gets the other kids to make fun of you, too. They call out "Who boy! Who boy!" to you whenever they see you. They do not stop at doing it on the bus. They taunt you in the hallway, at lunch, and on the playground. They mock you when the teachers are not looking.

Once you bravely told Frank to stop teasing you—just like your parents suggested you do. He made sure the bus driver was busy, and then he gave you a good shove.

Frank and his friends laughed at you when you cried.

You did not tell your parents because you did not want to upset them. They fight a lot lately and you fear they will fight over this, too.

Looking out the window of your classroom you often wish that, like the Doctor, you had a TARDIS and could time travel back to last summer. You would like to go back to hanging out on the front porch swing, reading about rocket ships and otherworldly adventures.

No one at school knows that you—a kindergartner—can read books without pictures. No one taught you to read. You figured it out on your own. You do not know for sure, but you think that either no one would believe that you read that well or the kid on the bus would tease you about the hat *and* the books.

You decide it is best to just stay quiet and hope that next year your life will get easier.

* * *

Finally, imagine you are a parent, a woman named Claire.

Your youngest child was a handful from the get-go. Colicky, rowdy, prone to meltdowns—with her infancy and toddlerhood, you knew you were done having kids.

As she grows, she requires you to call upon increasingly agile parenting skills. She can be high strung, intense, argumentative, and emotional. She is prone to throwing herself on the sofa, the hardwood floor, even the ground in the backyard when she gets revved up.

Recently, your new occupational therapist sent you your daughter's test results: Sensory Processing Disorder (SPD). Noises, sounds, and ordinary stressors easily overwhelm her. When this happens, she can throw a mean punch—a fact that has landed her in serious trouble and resulted in your decision to homeschool her.

You have had her tested for other things in the past. SPD makes sense and explains so much about her except for the high intelligence. You know that, like you, she has a very high IQ.

Unlike you, she struggled to find her rhythm in public school.

When you quit your corporate job and pulled her from school, your partner thought it was strange to homeschool just her. So, you brought your older kids home. Your first three kids, the ones who relished academics (like you had done), fell into an easy routine. Your youngest daughter did not. "Homeschooling is awful," she said several times, tearing up a workbook when she missed one math problem out of the ten she had otherwise answered correctly.

Your other kids also excelled immediately in the new co-op that you joined midway through the school year in order to provide social opportunities. Your youngest remains miserable, mostly because the mothers kept insisting upon bringing festive, nut-laden treats that she could not enjoy due to a severe nut allergy.

Reading late one night you encounter a blog post by a mom frustrated by the fact that she and her child had to leave a homeschool co-op because her child with Asperger's Syndrome was tormented and teased by the other kids. The story hits home. A human resources manager by training, you are frustrated that there is no proper system for dealing with conflict in the co-op. The more you think about it, the more it irks you that every week you have to calm your upset child who feels disappointed that she cannot enjoy the fancy goodies.

Your kid is unhappy. The world seems compassionless.

You? You are just plain tired.

Chapter 1

Bullying and the Gifted Lifetime

All children are affected by bullying, but gifted children differ from other children in significant ways. ~Jean Sunde Peterson[1]

In 2006, Peterson co-authored with Karen E. Ray a landmark study of 432 gifted eighth graders in 11 states. The research team asked students if they had, in their previous years of education, experienced bullying. The aggressive behaviors reported included all three major forms of bullying: verbal, physical, and relational.

Published in *Gifted Child Quarterly* (50:2), the study revealed that 67 percent of the students had been bullied (mostly verbally), 29 percent had struggled with violent thoughts about their experiences, and 28 percent admitted that they had bullied someone else. The students reported bullying peaked around sixth grade, with more males asserting they had been victimized physically. More females stated they had experienced relational aggression, a cluster of actions including rumors and social exclusion commonly referred to as "mean girls" behavior.

In an April 2006 news release announcing the study's results, Peterson cited improved communication between parents, educators, and students as crucial to helping gifted kids dealing with (or delivering) bullying. She said,

Studies have shown that when school counselors are involved with students and parents, great things can happen. We're hoping for a cosmic shift in the way schools see bullying, and we're hopeful that

counselors, teachers, and administrators can agree on how to identify and respond to bullying, just as we've been taught to identify and respond to sexual harassment.[2]

Those are noble goals.

Yet, like educators, aren't parents, sibling, grandparents, aunts, uncles, and guardians invested in the well-being of gifted kids? Don't they also deserve information and tools to help identify and address bullying? Not only are family members often the first to detect something wrong in a child's social setting, but relatives also play central roles in helping children and teens to resolve and recover from bullying incidents. What can (and should) families do to help young gifted people? How can they foster resilience and personal growth in the wake of bullying?

The Bull's Eye

It may be helpful if we think of a victim of bullying as being at the center of an archery target, with family members in the rings closest to the center. This means close relations can experience powerful emotions (anger, frustration, isolation) about the experience, too. Parents and guardians may feel insecure and unsure about what to do to help their child. With gifted families in particular, these complex emotions come on the heels of years of passionate educational advocacy and research on behalf of their children. Therefore, feelings of parental overwhelm and compassion fatigue can manifest.

A rising number of parents are opting to homeschool their gifted children who struggle to find a good social and/or academic fit in a traditional school setting. Unfortunately, although homeschooling gifted children may provide a range of benefits, home education should not be seen as a universal bullying panacea.

Bullying is not solely a school or community problem, per se. Bullying fundamentally represents a problem of broken human connection. As such, it can happen anywhere and anytime people come together, including homes and neighborhoods.

If gifted kids experience bullying differently, then we owe it to them to figure out how and why their experience differs. We also owe it to them to come up with strategies to help them succeed socially while minimizing pain and frustration.

This book, a first step in that process, draws upon experiences shared with me during the last two years by over 100 parents and other gifted advocates. With their help, we can put faces to the problems Peterson and Ray described in 2006. By talking candidly about our experiences as parents—and as former "gifted kids"—we open the door to improving and enriching our lives.

For starters, take the child in the first vignette of the prologue. I know her story well. That gifted girl targeted by a band of mean girls over and over again for years was me.

"Gifted"

It's such a loaded term, isn't it? Love or hate it, "gifted" is the word with which we must work on these pages. Why? Because it is the word educators use to describe a certain type of neurological difference, one marking some of us as cognitively and/or creatively distinct from "the norm."

Before the start of fourth grade, thanks to test scores administered by my school district, my parents received a letter branding me as academically gifted. In truth I wasn't "just" gifted; I was twice-exceptional ("2e"). The 2e term came into usage later than gifted, but it denotes, in my case, that I was both intellectually gifted and "something else" that made school and other learning and social settings challenging for me at times.

My bonus exceptionality was that thanks to some funky internal wiring, I was naturally anxious and socially awkward. (Truthfully, I still feel this way, but, with practice and concerted effort, I have learned to manage those feelings better.) I also have mild-to-moderate Obsessive

Compulsive Disorder (OCD) and likely had undiagnosed sensory processing issues in childhood.

Academically I was an asynchronous learner in grade school. In other words I was several years ahead of my age mates in one cognitive area (the humanities: writing, reading, and history), but held on to my grade level in math. In those days, educators were uncertain what to make of this contrast in degree of skill, and I was booted from my school's gifted program for not being "universally" gifted. Today we know asynchronous ability is not unusual for gifted kids. Thanks largely to the Columbus Group (a cadre of counselors and gifted advocates who declared asynchrony as integral to the very definition of "gifted"), top-notch educators now make accommodations for it in classrooms and programs.[3] Still, children struggle with uneven strengths and may feel perpetually out of synch with their peers as a consequence.

In the quest for optimal social development in gifted children and teens, sensitivity to their vulnerabilities and asynchronies (especially with regard to social skills) requires consideration, modification, and intervention. Given what researchers, educators, and gifted advocates are learning about the intersection of bullies and gifted kids, I see my twice-exceptionality marked me as easy prey for covert aggression, another term for relational aggression.

Also complicating matters were my *overexcitabilities*—inborn intensities and sensitivities in response to stimuli, common traits within the gifted population first described by Polish psychologist and psychiatrist Kazimierz Dabrowski. He determined some people are born with intensities and sensitivities in five areas: psychomotor, sensual, emotional, intellectual, and imaginative. When very pronounced, these overexcitabilities ("OEs") can yield, for better or worse, a more complex experience of life than the general population.

In my case, I had a mix of several OEs, but my emotional reactions to stimuli were especially strong. People were constantly telling me to "calm down" or remarking that I was "too sensitive." I internalized this feedback as a belief that there was something inherently wrong with me. This only fed my anxiety, which in turn led to discomfort in my body, heart, and mind that took decades to bring to heel.

Now and Then

Mind you, I am not suggesting that the kids (and a couple of adults) I knew in the 1970s woke up every morning and thought to themselves, "I'm going to bug that girl today because she's smart and gets worked up easily. It'll be fun to watch her cry."

What prompts people to bully is just as complicated now as it was nearly forty years ago. Bullying behaviors are learned either directly through role modeling by grown-ups or indirectly from a failure by adults to instruct children on proper, healthy, constructive social skills. Some children who struggle with emotional, psychological, or neurological disorders may also engage in bullying because of their social deficits.

The aggression many of us experienced back in the 1970s and 1980s at the hands of our classmates was no different than what many children face today—shoving, hitting, intentional social isolation, name-calling, shaming, shunning, and other degrading behaviors. The same could probably be said of the 1770s and 1880s.

Thanks to the work of counselors, psychologists, and other experts who study interpersonal behavior and its impact upon humans, here in 2015 we have a deeper understanding about what constitutes healthy pro-social behaviors. When I was growing up, the word "bully" was only ever applied to physically aggressive boys. There was no talk about covert or relational aggression being problematic, let alone hurtful. There just was not a lot of nuance around the topic.

Despite generational similarities, we must acknowledge one major distinction between bullying past and present: cyber bullying. Online relational aggression makes the major nightly network news shows with regularity here in the twenty-first century, usually in the form of hair-raising stories about kids tormenting peers on social media. Cyber bullying plagues young people, beginning as early as elementary school and continuing sometimes into early adulthood. It can be especially hard to extinguish due the fact that online bullies often hide behind fictitious usernames.

The Information Age has, however, brought some positives to the bullying problem. For instance it gives adults like you and me who want to teach optimal social skills a means of exchanging best practices. Parents, educators, and young people themselves can research and develop better ways to address bullying using blogs, e-books, and social media. Working together we can take and adapt concepts and parenting strategies derived from cultures around the world to fit our needs. We can also stay on top of important scientific and educational research and share it via social networks.

Conflicts and Friendships

"Don't kids need to learn to deal with their own disputes?" you may wonder. "Isn't interpersonal conflict part of growing up?"

Indeed, psychologists and educators tell us that feelings of isolation and rejection are normal during childhood, especially as children learn to navigate verbal and non-verbal social cues. Mature friendships are rooted in personal social skills sets built over several years. Some kids develop these skills faster than others. Trial and error is part of this process. The majority of children do not fully develop friendship skills until puberty.

For better or worse, childhood conflicts help establish and reinforce cultural and social norms. Through those early conflicts we learn how to resolve problems and follow the "rules" of social order.

Typically the line is crossed when physical or social power—or a perceived imbalance of powers—is a factor *and* the aggression is repeated (or promises to be repeated). When power is an issue, the word "conflict" is no longer appropriate. It is bullying, and it is not "normal." This power can take a number of forms, but we must remember the social kind—the type of power wielded like a sword by manipulative little girls and boys— can be as painful to the body and mind as a punch on the jaw.

Scientific research, counselors, news reports, and personal anecdotes tell us bullying *hurts*. The pain lingers, festers, and poisons relationships and minds. It impedes our concentration as well our motivation to learn, with potentially significant long-term effects. Indeed, bullied kids are prone to school absenteeism and have higher dropout rates. A 2015 study of over 5,400 children published in *The Lancet Psychiatry* revealed that bullied children suffer more long-term mental health problems in early adulthood than peers who only suffered maltreatment at the hands of adults.[4] The study came quickly on the heels of one from Duke University demonstrating that bullied children are more apt to experience harmful tissue inflammation in adulthood, with potentially serious health consequences.[5] Together these two reports have major implications for educators, health care providers, and families.

What about those kids who are extra-sensitive to bullying, the kids who cannot just walk away and "shake it off"? As Peterson and others have noted, some gifted youth seem hardwired to pick up—and react against—social injustices. Might these children be more apt to internalize their upsets in the form of anxiety or depression? Are these kids more likely than peers to have higher C-reactive protein tests indicative of elevated levels of inflammation in adulthood? There are no clear answers yet, but these are the kinds of questions up for consideration by experts.

We do know that children who lack emotional regulation skills (perhaps resulting from ASD, SPD or ADD/ADHD) can over-respond to an incident with physical violence. With help identifying bullying and coaching in how to address it, however, the vast majority of children can learn to regulate their reactions and hopefully minimize long-range mental and physical health impacts.

Who gets bullied—and why? Some bullies pick a target simply because they do not like the cut of the other kid's jib, but the children most vulnerable to bullying are targeted for standing out in some way.

Bullies can target victims on the basis of the color of their skin, the way they roll their Rs, the fact they cannot eat peanut butter or dairy, or how poorly they perform in team sports. Within the last twenty years, studies have revealed that children with significant disabilities are especially prone to being bullied. A 2008 study in the *British Journal of Learning Support* found that 60 percent of disabled students were bullied. This is in contrast to 25 percent found in the general student population.[6] Curiously, the percentage of disabled students estimated to be bullied in the British report is remarkably similar to the 67 percent of gifted kids who had been targeted, as mentioned by Peterson and Ray. Social interaction when you live outside the margins of "normal" can be treacherous.

Clear, Easy Targets

In contrast with the 1970s and 1980s, a greater number of gifted educators, parents, and advocates today are aware of the fact that children and teens can be bullied solely for being smart. Oh, sure, in the 1980s we had the *Revenge of the Nerds* comedy film franchise that capitalized on the jocks-mocking-geeks trope, but I do not recall anyone ever taking that sort of behavior seriously. The behavior was framed—and dismissed—as "boys being boys."

Most thoughtful, competent parents seek to help our kids move beyond bullying behaviors in constructive ways. Loving parents want to refine interactions for the benefit of all children. This is not to suggest we want them to be unchallenged. We understand that growth often comes with challenges. What we crave for our families is a higher standard of interpersonal relationships between peers and within our communities. If we have very sensitive, emotionally intense gifted kids, we want to help them feel less frustrated and have greater self-assurance if they are targeted. Likewise if our kids are tempted to become bullies—and gifted/2e kids can experience a desire to dominate others—we want them to redirect themselves before harming someone.

At heart all parents who are concerned about addressing bullying want the same things for our kids: quality interpersonal relationships and positive emotional growth. For this reason, it is time we began to share stories with our gifted/2e kids. Our youth (and their parents) need frequent exposure to examples of how life can improve as time passes.

To that end, I will divulge a little more about my own bullying experience.

One Gifted Lifetime

We moved to Paris, Texas, when I was four years old. My father was given a position at an industrial bakery and dedicated his energy to his work. Torn from the fabric of her family in Houston and dropped into a small Southern community that ran primarily on kinship connections, my mother was uneasy. As for me, I felt like a lonely outsider.

From early childhood, I had bouts of feeling uncomfortable in my own skin. I was a talkative, excitable child. According to family lore, I spoke sentences as soon as I could string together syllables in a coherent way. I was highly imaginative, writing my first, complete one-act play in grade school. Temperamentally I could vacillate between passive and bossy. Some teachers liked me and found me engaging. Others found me annoying and told me as much with body language. Nevertheless, like a lot of gifted children, I was more comfortable with adults than kids from an early age.

As a social misfit, I understandably loathed early elementary school. In the spring of my third grade a young, glamorous new teacher named Pat Clark (now Pat Bolton) arrived at our school and saved my soul by introducing me to the world of theatre. This became a passion for me until college, when writing became my greater interest. Although I had a creative outlet in place from late childhood onward, it took me until my sophomore year in high school to find a group of peers with whom I deeply connected. Most of them were two and three years older than me. They soon graduated and moved on.

Although I had friends throughout my teens, I silently experienced overwhelming depression, anxiety, and suicidal ideation during adolescence, especially between the ages of 15 and 19. The self-loathing I developed with the help of my grade school tormentors flourished silently during my teen years. It was not unusual for me to cry myself to sleep, listening to the grating voice within me repeat how I was unloved, unvalued, and unneeded. When I did move out of this phase, I made a common mistake: I engaged in a fair amount of relational aggression myself.

If you know and love a gifted child, elements of my story may sound familiar. Several of my own traits are common within the gifted demographic: marginalization, uneven social skills, preference for adults, asynchronous skills, vivid imagination, and intense emotions. Moreover, teens who were bullied in childhood or adolescence are at greater risk of suffering anxiety and depression or contemplating suicide. Some teens succeed at taking their own lives, with their family and community only coming to know the full extent of their pain after the fact.

In hindsight, I was lucky.

From Bullied to Bystander

Fast-forward with me two decades to parenthood. Blessed with a bright, spirited child in my mid-thirties, and having decided to work from home in order to homeschool him, I have spent a lot of the last decade on playgrounds. There I have watched adults and children succeed and fail at social interaction. Between this first-hand observation and the stories other parents have shared with me, I have been to the frontlines of the "mommy wars," female-to-female relational aggression that frankly bears eerie resemblance to the mean girls behavior of my youth. Peer-to-peer relational aggression—including cyber bullying—happens within adult social circles, too.

Especially frustrating for our family is rampant ignorance about food allergies. Our son is peanut allergic, and our family has encountered relational aggression directed at us for trying to avoid peanuts and peanut butter. Note that several researchers, including James Webb, have written about how gifted children have severe food allergies in higher numbers than the general population, a fact of life that complicates social interactions. Alas, for many gifted/2e families, a food allergy is another target for a bully to hit.

Thanks to my work as a gifted advocate and as the author of a homeschool book, I have learned quite a bit about the marginalization and shunning experienced by kids who are 2e, having dual diagnosis of giftedness together with Autism Spectrum Disorder (ASD), ADD/ADHD, SPD, OCD, or serious anxiety (to list only a few conditions). These stories are hard to hear. Sadly, while a rising number of parents of 2e kids are coming to homeschooling because of bullying issues, from what I have seen and heard firsthand, home education is not a magic bullet.

Bullying happens during homeschool play dates at well-organized homeschool co-ops, too. In fact, when he was six, our son had an unfortunate encounter during a homeschool art class held at a playground, where he encountered a physical bully who left him with an egg-sized bump on his forehead. The bully, a much older girl, had a shocking reputation, one that had followed her from another community several hours away. Other parents knew to steer their children clear of her on sight. I did not. She seemed fine to me. She also seemed very bright. She proved to be cruel, manipulative, and violent.

The experience left my son and me reeling for months as we both tried to recover from the myriad feelings left in the bully's wake: pain, isolation, fear, and regret. Within minutes I could vacillate between sheer rage at the perpetrator and deep compassion: *What could be going on in the bully's life that would result in that kind of behavior?*

Now I understand how my son's encounter acted as a trigger within me, bringing old memories of my own childhood pain to the surface. The experience was so shocking to me that I felt emotionally paralyzed in the hours after the event. I also felt incompetent and ill-prepared to aid my son in his processing of it.

With hindsight I see how, because I had never come to grips with my own experiences, I had not learned to manage my own emotions in the heat of the moment. Consequently, when my son was hurt, I was a less-than-effective parent. To this day I wonder if my own abrasive emotional reaction and the body language I displayed when I yanked him from the playground signaled to him that he was somehow at fault. It was one of my worst moments as a parent.

From Darkness into Light

In response to the incident, I absorbed every book and article available on the topic of childhood aggression. At the time there was a lot of good information to work with: books about trauma-proofing kids, socio-emotional skills development workbooks, conflict management strategies for kids, and stress reduction CDs. Missing from my late-night Amazon.com search results was the one, slender, nuts-and-bolts guide I most desired, the one with an overview of how to parent a kid who encounters bullying in *any* social or academic setting. Meanwhile, two big questions loomed large for me: *How can families work to stop bullying before it happens? How can we help our gifted and twice-exceptional children rebound from a bullying experience with minimal long-term fallout?*

Almost nine months after the incident on the playground, a close friend alerted me to a lively, emotional discussion about bullying on the Gifted Homeschoolers Forum Facebook page. "You need to take a look," she said. "These parents need someone to tell these stories."

I followed her advice and was blown away by what I found. Within a few minutes, a proposal for this book was en route to my publisher.

About this Book

On the remaining pages of this text we will explore in greater depth what we brushed over in this chapter, including: what marks gifted/2e youth as targets for bullying; the impact of bullying upon kids, teens, and their families; what makes some gifted/2e individuals prone to bullying; and, finally, how parents and other gifted advocates can help restore a sense of social connection

In preparation for this book, I strove to synthesize my research into something informative, useful, and respectful of all parties. This includes the 100-plus families of gifted/2e kids who have so generously volunteered to share their stories with me via my non-scientific survey instrument, emails, and conversations. Perhaps when presented as a group, these anecdotes and observations can help educators and mental health care providers understand how and why gifted/2e individuals merit extra consideration when bullying occurs.

Before we dig into the stories of families whom I have encountered in the last two years, I need to introduce you to someone whom you likely never anticipated encountering on these pages.

Ladies and gentleman, Mr. Elvis Presley.

Chapter 2

Elvis and Eve

Bullying is not about anger. It's not even about conflict. It's about contempt—a powerful feeling of dislike toward somebody considered to be worthless, inferior, or undeserving of respect. . . . In other words, bullying is arrogance in action. ~Barbara Coloroso[1]

Shortly after my paternal grandmother gave me a collection of his greatest hits for Christmas, Elvis Presley died at his Memphis home, Graceland. He was 42, and the death was attributed to an overdose. This tragedy followed years of reported prescription drug abuse and mercurial interpersonal relationships.

That was 1977. I was almost seven years old, and I vividly remember the evening news reports on the day he passed away. Imagine my surprise in 2013 when I found Elvis smiling up at me in a Texas nursing home.

Elvis, Eve, and Me

For several years, my mother has resided in a Central Texas nursing facility. Old, small-town nursing home rooms tend to be small and cramped, similar in layout and scale to classic college dormitory rooms. Mom's room is no exception.

It was across this space that I first saw "Eve." Newly released from the hospital, she had carved out a place of honor for The King of Rock and Roll on her tiny bedside table. A large frame showcased a black-and-white, 8x10 publicity photo of a young, slender Elvis. The photo bore the dedication "To Miss Eve."

Hoping to spark conversation with her, I introduced myself and promptly asked how she obtained the glamorous photograph.

"Oh, I knew him growing up, back in Tennessee," Eve replied, pulling herself up a little straighter on the inclined bed. "He used to pass by our house every day on the way to school. They treated him awfully there, at the school. The kids did not like his music, his flashy clothes, his hair, or his guitar. His mother had to walk him to school. It was dreadful what they did to him, just for being different."

We continued talking for a few minutes about Elvis, and she shared what she knew about him as a child. As we talked, I was struck that the memory of someone else's bullying experience still troubled a little old lady—a neighbor, not a relative—over half a century later.

A quick online research confirmed Elvis had been bullied physically and verbally. The behavior continued for years, the bullies motivated by everything from his obvious talent to his curious looks and fancy clothes. In the words of one childhood friend, George Klein, who met Elvis after his family moved to Memphis:

> *He hadn't grown into his good looks yet so most Humes [High School] girls weren't sure what to make of him. As for the boys, they felt someone so different deserved to be punished.* [2]

Reading Klein's passage I thought of several families with gifted children I have come to know—especially the ones who were determined to express their authentic selves.

Indeed, as I reflected upon Elvis and Eve, I saw that there were a number of big lessons to be learned from the two of them. Taken together, their stories help us better understand the enormous social pressures exerted upon certain subsets within the gifted population, individuals who are especially vulnerable to bullying. They also hint at the impact bullying can have upon casual bystanders.

Was Elvis "Gifted"?

Without question, Elvis was a high-achieving person who behaved on stage in a manner in opposition to then-social norms. The music he introduced to the world became revolutionary. But was he "gifted"? The answer depends upon how closely one adheres to the idea that "giftedness" is solely about IQ points and academic prowess.

Like a lot of kids gifted (especially those in the arts), Elvis appears to have struggled academically. Several biographers describe him as being emotionally intense, another marker of giftedness. Klein writes of his friend as being "one of the smartest men I've ever met, and his deep, natural intelligence is something that doesn't get discussed nearly enough."[3] By entering an adult field early—Elvis played professionally in bars as a teen to secure money for his impoverished family—he was certainly prodigious vocally and with his instrument of choice, the guitar.

Early musical talent alone was enough to draw out school bullies circa 1950. We have an old saying in the South: "He's gettin' too big for his britches." The implication? The person in question is full of himself, perceived as haughty, and needs to return to his proper place in society. In short, he needs to change his behavior to fit societal expectations.

If you have read extensively about giftedness and gifted advocacy, then you have likely encountered the phrase "cutting down the tall poppies." It is a pejorative phrase found in the United Kingdom and Australia and used to describe how people with obvious talent or intellectual prowess are resented for being distinguished among their peers.

"Too big for his britches" and "cutting down the tall poppies." They are a curious pair of phrases, worlds apart, both of which reflect a human impulse to regulate through social pressure the behavior of others. The phrases have different precise meanings, yes, but both carry the same warning: "You better stay in line, kid, or prepare to suffer the social consequences."

Given the time and place in which he grew up and first asserted his distinctive character and talents, Elvis was a poppy ripe for the cutting. From what I have learned about his story—and having grown up as a Southerner myself—I will bet at least one person accused Elvis of being too big for his britches. Fancy hair? Clothes? Those were unconventional choices for a Southern boy back then.

One cannot help but wonder if verbal condemnation of Elvis by Tennessee adults in the 1940s and 1950s was seen as validation for the physical behavior of his schoolhouse bullies. Children learn norms about behavior from adults (teachers, neighbors, senior family members) via words and actions or from the absence of swift correction of inappropriate action. Belittling words and gossip from grownups—including derision of smart and talented kids—can plant the seeds of contempt, scorn, and hate.

Pushing Back on Social Norms

Without a doubt, young Elvis challenged social convention in the conservative, conventional Deep South. From an early age he wore outlandish clothes, grew sideburns, and toted his guitar around. Despite pressure from others, he was intent on standing out and being his own person.

How many of us parents of gifted/2e kids have experienced curious looks from strangers when our children have insisted upon wearing unconventional attire publicly and repeatedly—be it superhero costumes, fairy tutus, or Star Wars Padawan robes? Now, who among us would have said before parenthood, "No child of mine will just wear whatever he or she wants!"? Who among us has learned the hard way that personal preference can be especially pronounced in young, strong-willed gifted/2e children?

And then there are the sensory-sensitive gifted kids—the ones with touch issues that render socks, belts, buttons, zippers, and certain fabrics off limits. Parents of sensory-challenged kids spend large amounts of money on special compression garments and vests. These are supposed to look stylish, but worn frequently they can mark a child as "different."

A lot of us parents struggle to help our kids find the right fit in the social sphere. Sometimes these efforts work. Sometimes they don't. As parents of gifted/2e kids—specifically those kids who resist buckling down and conforming to social and academic metrics—we learn to choose our battles. Occasionally we make the uncomfortable choice of doing this in the face of disapproval from mothers-in-law and our closest friends.

Well into the teen years and early adulthood, parents of gifted/2e kids can struggle with their child's counter-culture tastes and unique physical, psychological, and emotional needs. And to think—all these eccentricities pop up alongside strikingly advanced intellectual prowess or artistic ability. Couple those with debate skills rivaling any trial lawyer and some exhausted parents find themselves thinking, to borrow the words of my friend, Jen Merrill, "I had no idea it was going to be this hard."[4]

Swivel Hips and Sexuality

As Elvis matured through adolescence into adulthood, his clothing and hairstyles veered at times toward the androgynous. Later in his life he wore flamboyant outfits with sequins, some as flashy as any Vegas showgirl's costume. His swiveling hips—signature pelvic moves that would bring condemnation as his star rose—were considered dangerously sexually provocative at the time. Rumors swirled about his sexuality before and after his death, though his documented public life indicates he identified as a heterosexual male.

Society can exert intense pressure against children and teens who defy conventional gender roles—be it through atypical dress, speech, behavior, or sexual orientation. These are important topics for adults to understand and address, even if it makes us uncomfortable. However, the earlier a child expresses his or her difference from the social norm publicly, the sooner bullying (both peer-to-peer and adult-to-child) may start. In the words of one parent of a gifted child struggling with gender identity issues, "[my child has] dealt with a range of responses to his own gender non-normative presentation, from simple mistakes [with gender-specific pronouns] (which aren't aggressive in nature, but can be experienced that way because they are so common) to things like name-calling and being singled out."

It is vital in any discussion about bullying within the gifted community that we acknowledge some kids can be targeted because they experiment openly with their sexuality or gender identity. In *Gifted Children: Myths and Realities*, Ellen Winner touches upon earlier work by renowned psychologist Mihaly Csikszentmihalyi. She highlights specifically his researched-based observation that female visual arts majors in particular are prone to experimenting more freely with their sexuality than peers both within and outside the gifted community.[5]

Frankly, Csikszentmihalyi's research squared perfectly with what my professional colleagues and I witnessed among our university students studying visual arts in the mid- to late-90s. And, why not? Artists are inclined by nature and are frequently invited to call into question, through their formal university training, cultural norms and "play" with them. Why wouldn't an avant-garde perspective on the world play out in private lives and intimate relationships? Coming to appreciate this reality, this different perspective on the human experience, made me a better academic and career adviser to the population with which I worked.

We have only touched lightly upon the subject here, but in order for gifted advocates to truly take on the problem of bullying in total, any discomfort we adults—especially parents—have around the topic of human sexuality, sexual orientation, gender presentation, and cross-dressing needs to be shed. Why? We know these individuals are especially prone to experience bullying from early childhood through the teen years and perhaps beyond.

Cyber bullying in particular tends to line up with "slut shaming" and other attempts at degrading young women for their sexual choices. Likewise, we need to stay aware of the fact that young people who identify as lesbian, gay, bisexual, transgender, or queer/questioning (LGBTQ) are marked for and vulnerable to bullying, both physical and verbal. LGBTQ teens also have higher rates of substance abuse, suicide, and suicide ideation than the general population. These are important facts to keep in mind with all youth, including gifted/2e individuals.

"Gifted Cubed"

Elvis and Eve were born during the Great Depression in already impoverished communities. They shared another thing in common: Elvis and Eve were socially privileged *white* children living, learning, and playing at the peak of the segregation.

Today mainstream media enforces cultural stereotypes about gifted minorities. You have likely encountered the "nerdy Asian male" trope in films; he is often the smart first-generation-American kid with the pushy parents. Perhaps you recall Steve Urkel from the old "Family Matters" comedy show, the extraverted young black man who was bullied for his geekiness and overbearing nature. Fictional though these depictions may be, they do reinforce negative attitudes about smart children and teens.

Sometimes stereotypes obtain a veneer of "truth." For example, many in education circles hold a pervasive belief that black students underperform academically from fear of being shamed for "acting white." This idea is used to explain the gap in achievement between the school performance of white and black students. Interestingly, as Ivory A. Toldson, a Howard University professor and senior research analyst for the Congressional Black Caucus, wrote in 2013 for *The Root*, the issue is not about people shaming all bright black students but specifically the "nerdy" ones:

> *In my own research, I have noticed a "nerd bend" among all races, whereby high—but not the highest—achievers receive the most social rewards. For instance, the lowest achievers get bullied*

the most, and bullying continues to decrease as grades increase; however, when grades go from good to great, bullying starts to increase again slightly. Thus, the highest achievers get bullied more than high achievers, but significantly less than the lowest achievers.[6]

Toldson's comment dovetails with statistics elsewhere about bullying and the acceptance (or lack thereof) of highly and profoundly gifted children and teens. Absent from his insightful analysis is mention of twice-exceptional children, be they of Asian-American, Latino/a, Native American, or African-American descent (or any other underrepresented group).

Fortunately, blogger and gifted advocate Doresa Jen has coined a term to help us all understand the plight of 2e minority students: "gifted cubed." A dyslexic university professor and homeschool mom of three black and profoundly gifted kids, Jen has a unique perspective to share about racial and gifted identities. In early 2015 she helped create a GHF brochure for educators about "gifted cubed."[7] During a Twitter-based discussion called #GTCHAT in honor of the brochure's release, Jen shared several observations from direct experience:

- Society sends so many messages about what [gifted] □is supposed to look like—including what color, ethnicity, etc.

- Communities of color have cultural norms [that] don't always buy into the popular understanding of giftedness.

- Often kids who "look different" from others their age/level of ability are seen as misbehaving or even pathological.

- [Gifted people of color] have to know giftedness is an "and also" part of themselves, not a replacement of their culture/race/ ethnicity.

While their own parents may be aware of the intense, complex social pressures gifted-cubed children face, it is time the wider gifted advocacy community give them greater recognition and support. In so doing, we can help cut the risk of their experiencing bullying.

Bystanders and Zero Tolerance

By the time I met her, Eve had lived a full life. She had married, had children, and grown old. What made her experience of watching Elvis and his mother address bullying stick out in her mind decades later? One could argue it was a brush with fame and wanting attention for it, especially as a newcomer to a nursing home. But if Eve wanted me to know she had known Elvis once upon a time, she could have just said so and dropped the topic. She did not. She chose to bring up the bullying matter without knowing I was researching a book about it.

Memories of Elvis—particularly his battles with bullies—had stuck with her for decades. Why? As a child several years younger than Elvis, Eve was never in a position to speak up for him or to intervene. She was powerless. What she did was bear witness to his discomfort and the community's reaction. Until the end of her own life—she passed away shortly before this book was published—Eve remained outraged about how no one had ever resolved the problem for Elvis. It is a poignant reminder that the next generation of Eves desperately needs adults to address bullying swiftly and effectively.

As bullying expert Barbara Coloroso, in her profound text *The Bully, the Bullied, and the Bystander*, writes:

> *It's important that our children see us stepping in, speaking up, and taking a stand against injustices, be those injustices in the family room, the boardroom, the classroom, or the city streets. When we do more than give lip service to our beliefs, when we walk our talk, we model for our children ways to be that potent force in stopping the bullying.*[8]

Powerful words. Not only do we owe it to victims and bullies to resolve conflicts in a manner that holds people accountable and nurtures growth in everyone, but also we owe it to onlookers, siblings, classmates, and neighbors.

We would like to think "zero tolerance policies" do the trick in school settings. They do not work. Again, in the words of Coloroso:

> *The intent of these policies [in all 50 states] is laudable, but the singular procedure—one size fits all (that is, mandatory suspension or expulsion)—that many school districts have implemented is inflexible, harsh, and lacking in common sense.*[9]

Zero tolerance represents the failure of school systems to adequately address what is a social problem, a lack of connection, empathy, and compassion. Because of the complexity inherent to relational aggression, cookie-cutter approaches seldom work for bullies, bullies, or onlookers. As schools struggle and stumble to find clear bully solutions—alongside issues of overcrowding, standardized testing, and the implementation of Common Core standards, frustrated parents increasingly look for other education options, including homeschooling a child be it either temporarily or permanently.

Elvis and Gladys

Elvis's love for his mother, Gladys, is the stuff of legend. When his career took off, he famously purchased a pink-and-white Cadillac for her. Mother and son were said to have enjoyed a close relationship throughout her lifetime. According to Eve's memory of her neighbors, Gladys was the visible advocate for her talented only child. Eve did not recall seeing his father, although Gladys and Vernon Presley stayed married until her death in 1958.

One wonders if, in another time and place, young Gladys might have joined the ranks of parents who homeschool their gifted and talented children so they can focus on their strengths, including prodigious careers in the performing arts.

Although she loved her son, Gladys was far from a saint. She struggled with alcoholism later in life and reportedly worried about the condemnation her son received publicly for his provocative performances. Gladys was, like today's parents of gifted/2e kids, someone struggling to support an outlier child swimming upstream against prevailing cultural notions. One wonders what she might have done if the internet were around back then. Would she have found solidarity? Would she have gone to look for strategies and support for the social pressure her son faced?

It is tempting to think so.

Spend some time in web-based forums or pages dedicated to nurturing gifted and talented kids today and you will find the topic of bullying pops up every so often. Many parents feel frustrated, overwhelmed, and confused about how best to address the problem—and therefore seek input from peers.

As mentioned previously, it was one such discussion on the GHF Facebook page that prompted this book. Below are a handful of the comments from the discussion. All of them were generated in response to a community member's question about how to deal with a school bully. Together, these remarks provide a snapshot of the frustrations parents of gifted kids experience with this topic:

- *Don't think I can help much—in our case the bully was a teacher.*

- *Question: Can you talk to the bully's parents?*
  Answer: I tried this and was flipped off in the parking lot. Apple doesn't fall far from the tree many times.

- *It was our experience that the school pretty much just didn't care. They looked the other way.*

- *I was bullied, too. Not only from the kids at school, but from my own family. It affected me for life. I didn't want my kids to grow up feeling like that. That's why we homeschool. My kids used to come home from school all the time because they were "sick" and when they stayed in school they came home [feeling] horrible.*

25

- *When my daughter was in kindergarten last year, she had a third-grade boy bullying her on a daily basis.*

- *Both of my daughters were bullied . . . the last "isolated incident" was when my older daughter was stepped on (she was lying on the ground outside during recess) TWICE by the same kid, on purpose.*

- *In our case the teacher and the principal were the bullies . . . I had to fight every year over the IEP and appropriate supports for him. . . . He has been homeschooled for one year. . . . I have a smart kid who loves to learn and I really enjoy him and all the stress over what was happening to him is gone.*

- *My son was bullied and had stomach aches almost daily.*

- *At the risk of making everyone gasp . . . my son was bullied, and I threatened the bully myself . . . I also let him and the school know that as of this point, my son is permitted to physically defend himself.*

- *Yeah, I was bullied more for being different than for being smart, but my differences were an aspect of my intelligence, so there you go. In elementary school, I had trouble with my teachers and vice-principal, because I tested really high on all the standardized tests, but I struggled with math. I froze up and freaked out during the timed tests and hardly got any done, and they would make fun of me and tease me for being stupid about it, partially because they thought I was being deliberately slow, because my test results made them have high expectations.*

- *My son has been bullied by both peers and adults. Mostly because of his sensitivity . . . and this bullying has unfortunately happened at church youth groups. When my son was younger, he cried easily so for one bully in particular, punching my son to make him cry was all too common. Also, [my son] has severe food allergies and cruel children have been known to throw food at him [that] they know he's allergic to. An adult leader bullied my son over music choice once, forcing him to listen to music he didn't like on a road trip without giving him equal opportunity to share his music with the group. Now that he's older [fifteen], this type of behavior doesn't happen anymore but I think that* ANY *difference can make you a target for bullies because that's what bullies do.*

What are we to make of these stories? What do they reveal about the unmet needs of smart families when facing bullies? Looking at them in 2013, I saw bold examples of both constructive and destructive choices. I also saw hints at larger themes faced by parents of gifted kids.

My next step two summers ago was obvious: ask parents more questions about their experiences and what they learned from them.

Chapter 3

Bullying Stories from Families

The bully, the bullied, and the bystanders—chances are your child is involved one way or another in this daily drama. ~Barbara Coloroso[1]

In popular vernacular, the word "bullying" covers a range of behaviors. Consequently, there is a great deal of slippage around the use of the term. "Bullying" is a lot like "gifted": we each seem to have different working definitions.

Experts are more precise in their language than the general population, however, and the distinctions they make are important, especially as we delve into a deeper examination of what gifted families have to say about bullying. As Eileen Kennedy-Moore wrote for *Psychology Today*:

Researchers have a very specific definition of bullying: Bullying involves deliberate, aggressive acts targeting a particular individual repeatedly, over time, (although some researchers also count a single severe aggressive act), AND it involves a power difference between the bully and the target. In other words the bully is bigger, stronger, tougher, or more socially powerful than the person being bullied, which makes it difficult or impossible for targets of bullying to defend or protect themselves.

A lot of what children call bullying is really just ordinary meanness, because there's no power difference.[2]

Power. Power is what separates bullying both from ordinary meanness and, as we saw earlier, run-of-the-mill interpersonal conflict.

This is an important concept because ordinary meanness, although frustrating, is not usually an intentional threat to anyone's health or safety. Sure, it can be annoying, uncomfortable, and upsetting. And for kids who already feel marginalized because of their personalities, emotional intensity, extreme intelligence, race, or sexual orientation, ordinary meanness can be especially aggravating.

Teaching our children to recognize and deal with ordinary meanness requires our helping them build up their frustration tolerance, specifically their ability to withstand social stress. We can teach kids to "shake off" or "blow off" a minor slight from a friend or a sibling. We can help them address ordinary meanness by teaching basic conflict management skills. (We will touch upon some of those strategies later in the book.)

It can be helpful to think of interpersonal conflicts as existing on a continuum. At one end is ordinary meanness: a casual bit of roughness in behavior or speech that ends with everyone moving back to normal, ideally after the aggressor apologizes or makes amends to the victim. In ordinary meanness, the aggression is primarily peer-to-peer. As we move across the continuum, power becomes a factor and we can start to speak of "bullying" in a way that matches up with what experts describe. First, we encounter covert aggression, also called relational aggression, or repeated acts designed to harm one's social status, relationships, or reputation. This is milder verbal bullying that, on the continuum, precedes full-fledged harassment and acts of physical aggression.

Looking at the continuum we can see how repeated acts of meanness—especially by other children who have greater social clout than the victim—can become something other than "normal" behavior. The boundary between ordinary meanness and covert aggression can be murky at times, but it is a critical distinction to make.

Mean Girls and Boys

Thanks to the popularity of the 2004 fictional movie *Mean Girls* written by comedienne Tina Fey, the phrase "mean girls" has become a household catchphrase. We must not forget, however, that Fey's inspiration—parenting educator Rosalind Wiseman's 2002 book, *Queen Bees and Wannabes: Helping Your Daughter Survive Cliques, Gossip, Boyfriends, and the New Realities of Girl World*—was a ground-breaking work for parents, educators, and students alike. Although the movie enjoys a wider fan base, the book, which sought to explain "girl world" to adults, has maintained its relevance over the years.

Recently, CNN reporter and editor-at-large Kelly Wallace interviewed Wiseman, among others, for a news segment and online article entitled "Mean Girls are Getting Younger." In the piece, Wallace cited Wiseman as saying:

> *Mainstream media is portraying girls at younger ages who are mimicking the worst of obnoxious, stereotypical girl behavior . . . rolling eyes, moving the hips around, being catty. So what girls are getting is that by eight or nine, this is sort of a 'normal' way to act.[3]*

Examples of such behavior cropped up frequently in the stories parents have shared with me within the last two years. One friend related a story about her lively, imaginative preschool-aged daughter being singled out as "weird" by a socially domineering peer, the daughter of a socialite. The experience left the little girl distraught—and her family stunned that their little girl was already experiencing mean girls behavior.

Another example of female-to-female aggressive behavior lifted from the survey responses:

> *My two gifted daughters experienced emotional/friend bullying. In each case my daughters became friends with another girl who manipulated them under the threat of "I won't be your friend*

if/ unless you _____." This happened before school, in the classroom, and on the playground. I found out from my girls after it had been going on for some time and they were emotionally distraught. The teachers had no idea until I informed them.

In recent years, Wiseman has expanded her research into the relational aggression patterns of boys. Her 2013 book, *Masterminds and Wingmen: Helping Our Boys Cope with Schoolyard Power, Locker-Room Tests, Girlfriends, and the New Rules of Boy World*, sheds light on the social world of boys, including why and how neuro-atypical boys with obvious social disabilities are often singled out and victimized. The most blatant example of this in the survey appeared in an anecdote from a mother of two gifted boys:

My second son is 2e and extremely emotion-centered. He would be verbally tormented by kids whom he [thought] to be friends, and eventually I pulled him out of a high-level elementary school in our current city. Boys would befriend, he'd give them his whole heart, and then they would take turns cutting him down verbally, making comments about him in front of him and to others that would get back to him. [They did this] in order to make him cry—since he does so easily. He tried going to teachers when it would start (usually at transitions or low-supervision times), but no changes ever occurred, and no kids ever got in trouble in the "zero tolerance" school. We are still dealing with the anger and hurt that came from those issues in grades K-2 . . . it is hard for him to trust male peers, although he trusts and gets along with adults.

Relational aggressive behavior frustrates families of gifted and twice-exceptional victims on at least four levels. On one, the behavior is "sneaky" (hence "covert aggression") and therefore easy for well-intentioned adults to miss. Children who are victimized may tell no one, including their parents. Indeed, the only signs of trouble can be sudden changes in behavior or complaints about school or other settings where the bullying occurs.

On the second level, covert aggression is tricky to address because no one can force another person to be nice. Obviously, no "zero tolerance policy" can be put in place for someone acting like a jerk. And frankly the fuzzy line between "ordinary meanness" and mean girls (and guys) can befuddle experienced educators when it comes time to address it with pupils.

On the third level, for a gifted/2e kid struggling to fit in socially—but standing out because of obvious differences—relational aggression is a proverbial punch in the gut, hitting them right where they feel most vulnerable. To the outside world, gifted kids responding dramatically to relational aggression (either by hiding or swinging a punch) appear "too sensitive." In truth, a good number of them are fed up with trying to fit in.

Finally, on the fourth level comes the fact that although we talk about relational aggression (which now includes cyber bullying), as a culture we do not regard or treat it as seriously as physical bullying. To their surprise, parents of victims may encounter friends and family who, upon learning about what a child is facing, dismiss frustration as "part of growing up." In other words, the sense of isolation and frustration the child feels can spread into the family unit, potentially exacerbating the problem.

Mean Grown-Ups

Sometimes, grown-ups who should—by their position of influence within a child's life—be clear-headed, compassionate stakeholders in the child's overall well-being can function as bullies.

From the online survey comes this parent's story:

In my daughter's third grade year, she and a friend were being severely bullied by another student of the same age. When my daughter and her friend went to the school principal for help, they were immediately labeled as "trouble makers." The bully was allowed to lie about her behavior, regardless of the fact that both of the other girls told a different story.

A behavioral agreement was set up. (These are usually reserved until much further down the line in severe behavioral challenges.) All of the girls were routinely watched by the principal—who was on the lookout for anything she considered "inappropriate."

My daughter became very, very worried about all the ways she might step out of line. She began playing alone, away from other students. Some of the other students discovered that she was afraid to respond. They took full advantage of this. My daughter was routinely accused of doing things that she did not do and was then routinely told that standing up for herself was "rude" and "talking back." She was routinely told that she was anti-social and had social issues.

My daughter thought that she could handle herself, and so much of this continued for months. My husband and I knew she found school "hard" and didn't really want to be there, but unfortunately we didn't realize just what was going on.

All of this came to a head when five fifth grade boys accused my daughter of throwing pinecones and rocks at them and "not allowing them to run away." I was called by the principal with this particular report.

My first question was, "How on earth could one, much physically smaller, third-grade girl stop five, larger fifth grade boys from leaving an area they didn't want to be in?" I decided to fight the accusation based on logic. . . . I was then given the explanation that my daughter is, according to the principal, "a problem child. She is a show-off in class, but she does not do the work she is supposed to do. She's perfectly capable of working above the grade level work, but she's sloppy and doesn't bother to care about spelling or other work. She has no interest in making friends and holds herself aloof from others."

As this story demonstrates, the right school fit for a gifted child is not just a matter of academic appropriateness. It is also a matter of finding a learning environment where adults understand and appreciate asynchronous development. Another parent wrote via the survey:

Our profoundly gifted/dyslexic/dysgraphic son was enrolled in a small, private lab school that advertised a loving, supportive family atmosphere. When we completed educational testing (privately) and our suspicions of dyslexia and dysgraphia were confirmed, we met with the first grade teacher in advance of school starting to talk about what we could do and what she could do to help. Initially she suggested that nothing needed to be done for either of his exceptionalities. She would, she said, take care of it. Our son was increasingly unhappy, though he was either unwilling or unable to tell us exactly why—it was boring, he was not learning, et cetera. We met again with the teacher and she said nothing could be done to help him. He would not be allowed to progress in math because he wrote too slowly, and she seemed surprised that taking away his recess because he did not finish his written work fast enough did not motivate him. When we finally withdrew him in the spring to homeschool him, we learned from our son that she regularly ridiculed him in class, and would often lean down to whisper to him, "You know you are not as smart as you think you are."

It is worth noting that the parents in both of these stories pulled the children from the school to begin homeschooling.

Ignorance and Insensitivities

Sadly, several parents shared with me other instances in which adults (teachers, family members, neighbors) were the bullies—or, more often, aided and abetted bullies. A recurring theme in these stories was the aggressive adult's stated belief that the gifted child, because of their intelligence, should be better able to handle what was happening to them socially.

This is an especially challenging problem to address, let alone resolve. It requires the aggressor be receptive to learning about giftedness and letting go of her obvious prejudice. Parental advocacy can only move someone so far. One frustrated parent, the mother of a child who developed post-traumatic stress disorder (PTSD) in second grade from bullying (after two years of school-stress-induced hives school), wrote how multiple educators told her "[if] he's so smart, he can save himself."

Frequently complicating these cases is general ignorance about twice-exceptionalities and their impact on the child's social skills set. Another example from the survey responses illustrates this phenomenon:

In preschool, he was physically pushed around by other kids. As he is extremely touch sensitive [due to SPD], he did not react well and thought they were hitting him very hard. He would react by pushing back. This was usually then interpreted by his preschool teacher as him being a bully, as he was not very good judging the level of his own physical strength.

He also will usually fall victim to teasing when he does sports with other kids, like karate and gymnastics. He does not react well to other kids breaking the rules and will get very upset. The other kids will then "push" the boundaries of following the rules a little to get a reaction. The teachers are quite oblivious, as the rule breaking is quite minor. As the lessons allow parents to observe [the students], it is really very obvious. He will also be pushed to the back of the line by other kids. He is not very physically adept due to his SPD . . . and his lower limb cerebral palsy."

In this story, the child is clearly twice exceptional: not only does he have SPD but also a movement disorder. Yet whenever we talk about 2e kids and their reactions to bullying, the topic quickly becomes more complex.

On the one hand, some twice-exceptional child are uniquely "more" in one or several ways at once—*more* sensitive to harsh words and actions, *more* introverted and extroverted in their response to conflict, *more* dedicated to social justice—than what we expect of school children. On the other hand, some twice-exceptional children can be "less"—*less* adept at basic social interaction, *less* invested in working out conflicts, and *less* attuned to how their own behaviors spark aggression in others.

In short, there can be a knotty, individualized set of problems to solve when working with twice-exceptional kids who are being bullied. While we have to tread carefully so as not to shame or blame them for their reactions, we also must accept that, in some instances, repeated rejection from others can be instructive. It may be helpful to explore openly with a child how mild relational aggression can be a valuable form of feedback on aspects of one's own behavior that need to be tempered.[4] With the aid of compassionate adults (including a team comprised of teachers, parents, coaches, and therapists), a sensory sensitive child can learn to restrain his reaction or find better means of addressing the problem than landing a punch.

Failure to teach any child how to regulate emotions and reactions, of course, can potentially result in the child becoming the aggressor more often than being a victim.

Power Grabs and a Rage to Master

If bullying is defined as a conflict between two people with uneven power, then it is inevitable that a few gifted kids are going to make a power play of their own and become bullies themselves. For some young people, the switch from defense to offense is made for survival's sake. In the words of Canadian blogger and gifted advocate Cara Martin, "If you're on the precipice between being bullied and being the bully, some kids will choose to be the bully to avoid being bullied themselves."

Basically, it is survival of the fittest out there in kid world, and gifted kids—especially those children who come up short in social skills, emotional regulation, and impulse control—may be at risk of learning how to crush others be with a barbed wit or, less commonly, a punch. This is not to suggest they are born "bad" or have a Machiavellian streak. Rather, as one parent noted, "A child who is driven to *do* something, anything, is going to make more missteps (including aggression) than a child who can comfortably wait for instructions before proceeding."

Interestingly, several gifted adults with whom I spoke acknowledged regretfully that they had been bullies themselves, some as late as their teens. According to them, the key factor in their behavior was arrogance—a tendency to overvalue one's intellectual prowess after years of being singled out as academically exceptional. Armed with a firm grasp of language and a desire to dominate others—from a need for revenge to a sense of gamesmanship—some smart children and teens prove to be cunning and stealthy in their skillful manipulation of the people around them, from siblings to parents as well as peers and teachers.

Frequently gifted children or teens come to be a bully over time because a need is unmet—be it social, emotional, or psychological. Understanding that needs are unmet in bullies, too, is an important step to resolving a bullying problem. This requires compassion, which can be hard to access when behavior aggravates us, disrupting home and school life. As Jade Rivera, an Oakland-area educator and consultant, wrote to me in an email discussion:

[Some gifted/2e children] have very little actual power in the world. It makes sense that they would use whatever they have at their disposal as they navigate this world full of negative judgment and open hostility towards their difference. Often the only defense is their voice. A highly verbal child will turn that voice into a dagger if she feels backed into a corner, prompting others in her life to label her as a "bully."

Based on anecdotes shared with me, the gifted children at the greatest risk for engaging in intentionally relational aggression and verbal bullying are highly verbal individuals. As Rivera noted, they "may find that their biting wit is the only defense they have in a world that doesn't understand them." Indeed some adults shared stories of how their own childhood aggressive behaviors resulted from defense mechanisms gone awry. They may have initially used harsh words to cut others down in self-defense. Once enthralled with the power they claimed in the process, they used hurtful words freely on innocent friends and family members. When there were no checks on the behavior, it continued. (Several people wrote to me about adult-to-adult relational aggression—a topic beyond the scope of this book. This suggests plenty of gifted adults are out there playing the domination game in homes and workplaces.)

As we saw earlier, twice-exceptional children with sensory issues can be prone to physical reactions (hitting, punching, slapping) when provoked. This can lead others to label them unfairly as bullies. Context for a behavior can be difficult for adults to see or prove. Without support and appropriate interventions, however, these children may attempt to live up to the bully label. Impulse control in a high-energy child with strong emotions can take years to bring under control, trying parental patience and taxing pocketbooks. In the meantime, the child can struggle to find social acceptance and understanding while continuing to act out in anti-social ways, including physical aggression, despite the fact that parents swear he or she "really does know better" intellectually.

The parents could be on to something. A 1998 study of schoolchildren led by Debra Peplar noted that the kids labeled as "aggressive" by teachers were seen to engage frequently in more antisocial *and* prosocial behaviors than their "non-aggressive" peers.[5] The sample was small (only 39 children in total), but it reflects parental reports about impulsive, high-energy gifted/2e children being "nice once you get to know them."

We cannot overlook a simple, important fact: the childhood behaviors parents and teachers choose to reinforce and reward through their attention and engagement shapes and forms later behavior. Resistance and repeated antisocial behavior gets a child attention, something for which she is starved. A vicious cycle develops. In the words of Peplar *et al*, "Within the elementary school context, social interactions with peers may both maintain and exacerbate the behavior problems of aggressive children."

Some parents of gifted/2e kids recognize this reality. When they see their child routinely scolded and berated for peer-to-peer aggression with no progress, many choose to withdraw their child from traditional school settings to homeschool, where positive behaviors can be reinforced and nurtured free from the social biases that engulfed the child in a school setting. No wonder some families come to see homeschooling as an academic and social reset button.

Silver Linings

Some of the themes of this chapter are upsetting to encounter, in part because they play into our biggest fears as parents: watching our kids struggle socially.

My research did have a few bright spots, however. Each involved adults (teachers, parents, counselors) who responded to a bullying situations and uneven social skills involving gifted kids with compassion/empathy, an emphasis on individual strengths, and the presentation of workable solutions. The most effective adults took into consideration all the facts in a given situation as well as any distinctive learning or social challenges. They worked carefully and patiently to bring about changes in behavior.

The following story, lifted directly from the survey responses, demonstrates what a kind, professional educator can do not only to help a child but also reassure parents that a problem is being addressed.

I was blown away by the response of the school. When I went to the school counselor [after a failed attempt with an inept teacher], she was amazing. I never imagined that I could feel that supported . . . She handles situations [like this one] with unconditional support to the victim and a compassionate, appropriate, psychologically supportive response toward the bully—on an ongoing basis.

She addressed all involved with faithful and thorough counseling. When there was an escalation [of the bullying] at the [end of the school year], she had no hesitation to go to the principal's office to affect the result needed. The bullying ended from that point on. She has . . . ensured that they do not cross paths in class four years in a row.

Whatever they said or did, the bully remains utterly silent to this day when he sees my son. [The counselor] has worked on an ongoing basis to ensure that my son has the tools to address any issues on his own. Not that she was abandoning him to these situations at all, but supporting him in knowing what to do and being an utterly reliable backing to him ongoing.

This school counselor is the model of an effective advocate and social coach, someone who has the needs of all parties in mind. Would that every school setting had someone capable of guiding children through a bullying crisis.

Yet one need not be an experienced counselor to guide a child through social challenges. Parents can learn and do so successfully, yielding surprising benefits even years later. As one parent wrote,

"[The] positive impact of [our bullying experience] is that we are much closer as a family, and we do a much better job of communicating with each other. My daughter has learned that when I say, 'How was school?' I really want to know the details. We've also learned not to wait when we hear there might be a challenge, socially or academically, we're right there. I have to be careful not to 'hover,' but my daughters . . . they say I do a pretty good job of letting them run their lives."

Bullying situations, you see, can be teachable moments for everyone involved, including moms and dads.

Chapter 4

School Bullying and Your Child

By the time a child reaches out to an adult, the vast majority of kids have been dealing with the bullying and trying to ignore it for a long time. The only thing that happens when you tell a kid to ignore the bully is that they no longer think you care or are capable of helping them. ~Rosalind Wiseman[1]

Most parents read deeply and extensively about bullying only *after* a shocking event or series of events triggers an alarm. Perhaps this is the situation in which you find yourself now. Therefore, let us take a brief look now at the four critical steps parents must take to address school bullying.

Step One: Safety First

In the event any child has been physically harmed (or is being physically harmed repeatedly) or has had her physical well-being threatened, safety obviously must be the top priority. This includes addressing the emotional needs as much as treating any physical wounds and separating both parties if necessary.

Alas, many kids are bullied but their families do not find out in time to offer help. Some children are forthcoming about their bullying experiences; others are not. Generally speaking, extroverted children are more verbal about social frustrations, while introverted kids are less so. Yet victims may react in a manner opposite from their typical behavior due to stress, anxiety, or fear. Therefore, an extrovert who suddenly becomes introverted (and vice versa) may be a parent's only clue that something is wrong.

Changes in behavior are important clues on which parents must follow up because any child who is bullied may be vulnerable to post-traumatic stress disorder (PTSD) and other long-lasting emotional wounds. This can occur in seemingly "minor" bullying incidents and with seemingly insignificant injuries. Do not force yourself or your child to go it alone. If your child is in a school setting, reach out to school counselors and consider therapeutic support with a trained, licensed counselor in your community, if necessary. There is no shame in seeking aid, and counseling can be one cornerstone for personal self-care and self-compassion (see Selected Resources).

If a child or teen comes to you with a bullying report, listen without judgment from the outset. Demonstrate your love and support in ways that feel comfortable for her. Reassure her calmly that you are supportive of her. As tempting as it is to explode with your own rage, this can be frightening for some individuals.

As we have seen, bullying is stressful to victims as well as parents and other bystanders. A few highly sensitive gifted children experience stress and trauma from merely witnessing a bully in action. For this reason, remember that bystanders deserve sensitive care and the chance to process what has occurred with the help of a compassionate adult.

Step Two: Mind the Law

Criminal activity must be reported to law enforcement officials as soon as possible. Such activities include the presence or threat of a weapon, a promise of physical harm or death, hate speech and harassment (including attacks related specifically to a child's race, color, national origin, sex, disability, or religion), sexual abuse, and/or illegal activity of any kind.

When it comes to cyber bullying, different locales have different laws and regulations. Most social-centered websites offer community members mechanisms for reporting cyber bullies. Use them.

It is worth noting that, when it comes to twice-exceptional children with diagnosed physical, emotional, or cognitive disabilities, United States schools are required by civil rights laws to address the problem. The StopBullying.gov website maintains current legal information related to discriminatory harassment, which covers several protected groups.

In the absence of illegal activity, managing behavior of underage minors primarily falls to supervising adults. With this role comes tremendous responsibility—and a need to maintain a level head.

Step Three: Calmly Work the Correct Channels

When bullying occurs within the context of a school or other educational setting (such as a church group or summer camp), parents are expected to alert representatives via the proper channels. In a public school, this process starts with the classroom teacher and runs up to the principal and through the superintendent to the school board. It demands parents demonstrate poise while being articulate advocates—perhaps in the face of understandably strong emotions.

School authorities should be the ones who contact the parents of other children. Unless you enjoy a close, personal relationship with the bully's family, resist the urge to reach out to them yourself. Also, refrain from using social media to call out suspected bullies and their families by name. This behavior has the potential to make the problem harder to resolve—and potentially more stressful for your own child.

As soon as you can, put down details of the incident (or incidents) in writing or in a special file on your smart phone. The act of writing helps keep us focused on facts rather than emotion. Jot down what your child or teen has revealed to you about the experience. In the case of cyber bullying, print out copies of hostile exchanges (texts, emails, social media posts) or photographs as evidence in case it "vanishes" when adults start to intervene.

Written and visual documentation are important tools for parents to use when addressing bullying in a school setting. This applies to how you report the original problem as well as how you manage your piece of the resolution process. Schools are based on organizational hierarchies that run on protocol, procedures, and written documentation. If you want to be influential within the system to protect your child, then you must work within that model.

Georgia school psychologist, Kathryn Rogers Grogg, Ph.D., shared with me a basic email template parents can use to follow up with school administrators after the initial report is made.

> *Dear _____:*
>
> *Thank you for talking (or meeting) with me on _____. (State the day and time of the meeting or phone call.) I spoke with you concerning _____. (Be specific about the names of all parties involved and include relevant dates when actions occurred.)*
>
> *My overall understanding of our conversation was _____. (Summarize the discussion.) You said the following actions would be taken by _____: _____. (Reiterate what was promised.) I said I would _____. (If you agreed to take an action or if you stated you would follow up with the administrator by a certain date, then put a reminder on your calendar to do it.)*
>
> *Please reply to this email to let me know that you've received it and that I have summarized our conversation correctly. I look forward to hearing from you.*

Dr. Grogg suggests that if there is no follow up with two business days, parents should resend the email, copying it to the next person up the chain of command, as well as to the school superintendent, the school board, and, if necessary, your Board of Education representative.

Step Four: Follow Up

Once a report is made, it is up to the school district to come up with an action plan for resolution and, if merited, punishment. Due to federal and state education privacy laws, the families of victims may or may not be made aware of the particulars of punishment.

In the event the problem resurfaces, parents must be at the ready to continue advocating for their child's safety and well-being.

Families of twice-exceptional children who qualify for special education under the Individuals with Disabilities Education Act may wish to revisit their Individualized Education Plan (IEP). Working collaboratively with teachers, parents can include strategies to address bullying. The Parent Advocacy Coalition for Educational Rights Center (PACER) hosts a National Bullying Prevention Center website (Pacer.org/Bullying) offering information specific to the bullying of children with disabilities. This can be useful in the IEP revision process.

If no satisfactory resolution to the problem occurs through parental advocacy alone, consider contacting a lawyer. By reviewing your documentation, rules, and laws, an attorney can help a family determine just how far and hard to press the district. Further action may include—in instances where harassment persists—involving the U.S. Department of Education's Office for Civil Rights and the Department of Justice's Civil Rights Division.

Of course, the vast majority of bullying cases will be resolved long before this point is reached.

Keep Focused on Who Matters Most

In the wake of significant bullying the emotional care of the children involved must remain a major focus. As parents, we may fall easily into the trap of fixating on our advocacy and therefore inadvertently overlook a child's emotional needs.

We simply must not forget that our young people deserve our personalized, appropriate care as they process what has happened.

Chapter 5

Nurturing Resilience and Healthy Relationships

The ways parents interact with their children contribute to shaping children's understanding of themselves, their parents, human nature, and the world around them. ~Inbal Kashtan[1]

While the bulk of mainstream media discussion hinges on what schools can do better to prevent bullying and address it when it occurs, research and anecdotes show warm, loving families and calm, reassuring home lives are of the greatest help to children who have been victimized.[2]

Still one may wonder: what specific activities can parents engage in with their children to ease upset and nurture resilience? As it happens, a variety of options may be tailored to fit individual needs, family dynamics, household budgets, and community resources.

Generally speaking, parents who shared their "bullying survival stories" with me—and who were satisfied with their results—focused their energies primarily on the basics: listening to their children and demonstrating concern, compassion and support; helping their kids address possible deficits in the areas of self-regulation (emotional and physical); and coaching them on social skills.

With the advantage of hindsight, parents shared significant revelations about their roles in relieving pain and building resilience. As one might expect, there were a mix of feelings. From the survey:

- *I definitely did not do as well with it as I might have. I did not realize some of it was going on until we were multiple months into it. I did not work to get as much information from my daughter as I should have. I learned a lot from this experience about talking with my child, and she learned a lot about talking with me . . . Looking back, I was struggling, trying to figure out what to do, thinking that we could find a way to make things work. I should have just said, "This is wrong," and brought it to a quick end.*

- *We sat him down and told him "But, J., you are weird. You are an amazing inventor. You program, you create. You think outside the box. You are weird. And a geek. And odd. And that makes you the most amazing J. I know. When someone calls you weird, say thank you! It isn't an insult when you embrace it." He did just that, and the would-be bully had no comeback. He couldn't hurt J. because the word had no power. We are all geeks. His dad is a programmer/computer nerd. I am a book nerd. His brothers are all geeks. This family watches Doctor Who, reads Harry Potter, looks up the genetics to their fish, and spends hours making code for Minecraft. We are weird and proud of that. We embrace it.*

- *I was worried for N. and felt like my job as a mother was to prepare her for a life of being lonely and misunderstood. I've had some life experiences in the meantime that have shown me I just need to be more intentional about finding the right kind of friends.*

- *We spoke with the teacher on several occasions. We also had our son see the counselor for a friendship group. Honestly the very best thing we did was not send our son back to public school. I have many friends that homeschool, so having a good, local support group has helped a lot. His behavior and attitude have turned around completely. He's made many good friends and is much happier overall. It helps to have support from online groups, as it helped our decision greatly. I had a lot of pressure from family to just make our son tougher somehow (they have no idea how sensitive he is) . . . Websites helped me understand that the sensitivity is part of who my son is, and time likely won't make it better . . . and more time with the bullying will just make it worse.*

- *I wish I had known more about giftedness and twice-exceptionality so I could have had more ammunition to [take] to the school meetings (where he was vilified, and we were told he was not creative because he liked to check out non-fiction books from the library). I wish we had moved him to a new school mid-year instead of trying to work things out. I wish I had listened to my mommy gut when both he and I would cry on the way to school. I wish we had found a counselor who understood giftedness earlier, so he wouldn't have had to go through trauma at school.*

- *Everyone seems to agree that bullying is wrong, but not many people react kindly to the child who is bullied. I often hear comments about him being too sensitive, immature, overreacting, weird, etc. My husband and I were also labeled as gifted during childhood and both of us were bullied. He handled it better than I did. We are trying to use our understanding to guide our own children in coping with these issues.*

Nurturing a gifted/2e child through bullying recovery may require sensitive, intentional, and long-term work on behalf of the parents. Several strategies and techniques recommended by real-life parents and counselors follow. Choose only the ones relevant to your family's needs, and be sure to review the Selected Resources section at the end of this book for further help.

When to Call a Therapist

Outside assistance in the form of counseling is an especially good idea if your bullied child has any signs of PTSD, which can include (but are not limited to):

- flashbacks of the experience (including nightmares or night terrors)

- emotional or physical distress when encountering something that reminds her of the event (a "trigger")

- avoidance of other people and/or difficulty with relationships

- trouble concentrating

- acting out

- substance abuse in older children and teens

One need not have PTSD, however, to be traumatized. And a victim need not experience severe, dramatic, violent bullying in order to feel traumatized. As counselors Peter Levine and Maggie Kline write in *Trauma-Proofing Your Child*:

> *Trauma happens when an intense experience stuns a child like a bolt out of the blue; it overwhelms the child, leaving him altered and disconnected from his body, mind and spirit. Any coping mechanisms the child may have had are undermined, and he feels utterly helpless. . . . Trauma can also be the result of ongoing fear and nervous tension. Long-term stress responses wear down a child, causing an erosion of health, vitality, and confidence.*[3]

Levine and Kline also note that a child's vulnerability to trauma depends upon several factors including "age, quality of early bonding, trauma history, and genetic predispositions."[4]

Families should consider all of these factors when determining how best to help children recover from bullying, including whether or not to enlist support, even temporarily, from trained professionals.

One need not wait for a problem in order to reach out for therapeutic support, of course. A compassionate therapist sensitive to the needs of gifted/2e children can help families deal with feelings of isolation related to a child's exceptionalities, nurture any social skill lags in a 2e child, and/or serve as a sounding board for life's frustrations. For a child struggling with physical or relational aggression, a therapist can help a family work through anger management issues and nurture social skills.

There are long-term advantages to hiring a therapist as well. The introduction of a trusted professional counselor early in life can reassure a child that other people in the world care about her, her needs, and her feelings. This may in turn help nurture self-compassion and kindness.

The best counselors and therapists are people who demonstrate care and concern while limiting visible judgment. They ask thoughtful questions as they coach their clients to make and act upon authentic, safe, and responsible decisions. They are effective listeners, and demonstrate their interest in a client with engaging body posture and eye contact.

Naturally, parents can adapt and employ these behaviors at home, too.

Creating a Culture of Kindness

Giftedness tends to run in families, but not always. Twice-exceptionality is more common in some families than others, but it is possible to encounter a gifted/2e child standing alone on a branch of the family tree.

Whatever the intellectual, emotional, and psychological makeup of siblings and parents, the challenge of ensuring individual needs are met and interpersonal boundaries are respected falls to parents. Parental failure on this front can result in frustration, frequent conflicts and displays of aggression inside and outside of the home, and the potential social marginalization of a child or teen. This can be dangerous and harmful situation, potentially more so than aggression encountered in schools.

Fundamental to any child's success in life is a home life where care is consistent, rules are clear and enforced fairly, and conflicts are resolved in healthy ways. In a home where bullying and relational aggression occurs between siblings, meeting conflicting needs can mean significant work by parents.

Parents managing complex interpersonal situations may want to look to books and resources to brush up on their own conflict resolution management and communication skills. With an emphasis on compassion, understanding, and thoughtful articulation of needs,

Non-Violent Communication (NVC) techniques work well for a lot of gifted/2e families, especially those with emotionally sensitive kids. Inbal Kashtan's book, *Parenting From Your Heart: Sharing the Gifts of Compassion, Connection, and Choice*, is an excellent introduction to the NVC approach.

Parents who research parenting strategies, including NVC, may decide ultimately to draw from several models. Remember: the only real expert about any given child is an engaged, loving parent. At the end of the day, the most essential aspects of parenting strategies and rules about behavior is that they be enforced consistently and be respectful of all parties. If you are trying to repair or improve your parenting skills, you can expect trial and error in pursuit of growth. Give everyone the gift of patience.

Sadly but not unexpectedly in my research, a few parents confided stories about adult-to-child bullying at home and within extended families. As with teacher-to-child aggression in schools, successful resolution requires the adult aggressor understand why the behavior is a problem and be willing to change. A professional, licensed family therapist may help with the resolution itself or by supporting the child's primary advocates (usually the parents, but not always) as they deal with conflict, enforce boundaries, and, if necessary, end harmful relationships before significant damage is done to a child or teen.

Self-Regulation and Mindfulness

As children grow, we expect them to improve their ability to manage their actions and reactions. Individual children make progress at different rates. Twice-exceptional children often mature in ways so distinctive (and sporadic), that parents are left frustrated. At the same time, highly sensitive gifted children who have no diagnosed learning or physical disabilities can struggle to respond to frustrations in healthy ways, often to the bewilderment of their families.

In other words, a family need not have a formal diagnosis or label in place to see the value in intentionally scaffolding or providing appropriate, additional, *temporary* support for a child's emotional growth. Rather than "coddling" a child, parents carefully apply an emotional scaffold with the intent that it be removed when the child is better able to manage her own emotions. For example, scaffolding may involve a set protocol for dealing with certain situations, including the parent pulling a soon-to-be overwhelmed child to the side and engaging her with a practiced calming process. In action, it is the difference between barking at someone to "calm down" and saying compassionately, "Honey, let's sit together and practice calming ourselves so we can work on the problem together." Warm, modest praise is offered for success, including incremental progress.

Eventually, much like a building under construction, the custom scaffold is pulled down as the child moves toward optimal self-regulation. Granted, some 2e children, especially those on the autism spectrum, may require help with soothing well into adolescence or beyond. The majority, however, will get better at it, although they may remain more intense than their peers.

One effective emotional scaffolding technique parents and counselors have referenced to me repeatedly is home-based mindfulness training. On first glance, "mindfulness" can look New Age-y and foreign on the page. Thanks to state-of-the-art technology, however, science is demonstrating that mindfulness work (activities like breathing techniques and meditation) can relieve stress and anxiety. This in turn helps us perform better in all sorts of frustrating settings. When we think mindfully about a problem and the emotions that it triggers within us, we can move more easily toward identifying workable solutions. Research shows over time, just as bullying can reshape the brain and consequently change behavior in negative ways, mindfulness can reshape the brain in positive ways. (See Selected Resources.)

Contrast mindfulness with its opposite, mindlessness. Mindfulness is about empowerment and a sense of self-control and regulation. It is also about self-acceptance, compassion, and being fully present in the moment. Mindlessness is aimless, heedless drifting. That may be fine for a vacation at the beach, but is not so useful when it comes to everyday living and social interactions.

Because mindfulness involves non-judgmental self-acceptance, it can be a vital first step toward acquiring proper coping skills. When we use loving self-compassion to first acknowledge our feelings and behaviors—and refrain from judging others or ourselves harshly for theirs—we make a bold step forward with our self-regulation. With practice, we can learn to minimize stress while increasing our tolerance of distress.

Mindfulness, at root, is about acknowledging our quirks and intensities and working *with* them. This kind of internal work can be a transformative tool for children and adults who are anxious or highly sensitive by nature. A counselor trained in dialectical behavior therapy (DBT), a specific type of mindfulness-driven cognitive behavior therapy developed by Marsha Linehan, and sensitive to the needs of gifted/2e children and teens can be of great help to families. (See Selected Resources for book recommendations.)

The scientific evidence in favor of mindfulness training as a cornerstone of emotional development is so strong now that a number of schools are turning to these strategies to dial down bullying. A fine example of this is Inner Explorer, a Massachusetts-based pilot program developed by Laura Bakosh and Janice Houlihan that launched in 2011 and is now used by over 60 schools in 16 states. Preliminary results of the program suggest that not only does mindfulness help reduce aggressive behaviors, but also it improves academic performance.[5]

Those results can, with time and practice, be replicated in home (and homeschool) settings. When parents practice these centering techniques with their children, the activity becomes a powerful means of fostering parent-child connection. There are a number of approaches available, and devout families can rest assured there are models (including contemplative prayer) that align with every major world religion.

Mindfulness training need not be complicated or expensive. Again, I have included several print and online options in the Selected

Resources section. Among them are books on basic, easy-to-learn breathing techniques described by authors like Thich Nhat Hanh and Meena Srinivasan—two of my favorite authors on the topic. By practicing regularly until these techniques become a reassuring habit, children may carry these skills into adulthood.

The next step up from mindful breathing practice is meditation. As with breath work, the practice of meditation can be secular or faith-based in nature. Either way, meditation helps to quiet the mind and improve impulse control while minimizing stress and its impact upon our bodies and minds. Meditation does require practice to master. Fortunately, there are a multitude of free or low-cost resources online, including videos, to help you get started. (GoZen.com and HeartMath.org are good starting points.)

Physical Regulation and Flow

Earlier this year, an old friend reached out to me with a question. She had just learned her twice-exceptional son was experiencing inappropriate, hurtful verbal aggression from a teacher. Understandably concerned for his well-being, my friend wanted to know what she could do over the next few days to help her child. We discussed her strategies with the school (as outlined in the previous chapter), and then I offered unconventional advice: get physical.

No, I was not suggesting she do something violent. Rather I recommended that she engage her child in an activity they could share, preferably one of his choice. It could be a short walk around the block, a shoulder massage, a quick game of basketball, or a light bit of yoga. (If the weather is bad or the child is feeling unwell, it could just be a long snuggle on the couch.) Whatever your child is comfortable with, physical activity enjoyed with a loving parent can help foster reconnection and reassure him that he is cared for as a human being. Making time for these kinds of activities in our hectic schedules help our children build a reserve of loving connection on which they can draw when life feels difficult.

In particular, the regular practice of controlled, repetitive, and rhythmic physical activities (yoga, tai chi, and various martial arts, for example) can be helpful and soothing. Yoga was a big help to me in my teens, and I have returned to it over the years. With practice, these pastimes help children and teens experience "flow," a vibrant mental state where one feels competent, in control, challenged, and self-fulfilled all at once. Psychologists like Mihalyi Csikszentmihalyi, who coined the term "flow," tell us it is an optimal experience of being human. As young people learn to induce this state through their own practice of a favorite activity, they can summon it to reduce stress and regain a positive frame of mind during or after a frustrating situation.

Martial arts in particular can be invaluable for children who struggle with emotional regulation. The physical confidence they acquire over time can be useful to ward off bullies. Plus, parents have the added reassurance of knowing their children are learning how to defend themselves in the event of a violent encounter. Our son has studied martial arts for three years now in two studios, one for Tae Kwon Do and the other dedicated to karate. In his classes I have witnessed firsthand the changes that can take place on the mat with a range of kids at different ages, including children with apparent twice-exceptionalities and strong overexcitabilities.

To incorporate flow-activating physical activities into your family's weekly schedule, take a close look at your community. Many YMCAs offer free or reduced-cost classes in yoga, martial arts, and meditation. If you live in a rural area, check your local library for books and videos.

Pause for Parental Self-Care

Taken together, emotional and physical regulation skills form the cornerstones of self-control. These are vital to fostering resilience as well as minimizing aggression in all its forms. We must not overlook the fact that emotional and physical regulation skills are important for parents to nurture within ourselves.

Indeed, the practices outlined above for children work as antidotes to compassion fatigue, a state of mind and being that can overwhelm parents beleaguered by raising gifted/2e kids while also dealing with grown-up demands and needs. Too often, adult emotional and physical needs in gifted households go unmet. Sometimes this goes on for months or years at a time with significant costs.

This is problematic not only for parents but also for the children, who look to us to model self-care and resilience. If we stay worn and frazzled, enraged and frustrated, or zapped and checked out, then our children learn those behaviors are acceptable for themselves. A vicious cycle develops, and problems of disconnection and frustration perpetuate. Mature, responsible self-care is a visible form of self-compassion, something we need to see more of in the world and in our families.

Social Skills Development Strategies

All children need social skills coaching sooner or later. Some kids just need more help, more often than others. For bullying victims as well as kids prone to physical and social aggression due to twice-exceptionalities (including ADD/ADHD, SPD, or ASD), long-running, heartfelt, and fact-filled discussions with their families about positive social behavior are useful.

Several parents have confided how researching topics related to bullying and then openly sharing what they learned with their children proved to be a powerful social learning tool. One parent, when asked how her family addressed their bullying problem, said in the online survey, "We read a number of books about relational aggression to become better versed in the terminology, which assisted us greatly in our discussions within our school community. Saying the right words is hugely important in these conversations." Obviously, these discussions can also be directed toward addressing sibling aggression.

Non-fiction books, videos, and television programs can help build a firm foundation for understanding how and why bullying occurs. Whether or not one homeschools formally, bullying curricula for schools can be adapted for home use. StopBullying.gov is a useful tool, as well.

In addition to talking about bullying specifically, it can be helpful to talk about social skills generally. Children who have significant social skills lags may benefit from the books and resources created by Michelle Garcia Winner, founder of the Social Thinking Center in California. Her website, SocialThinking.com, has a wide variety of materials suitable for home use.

Also, positive adult role models within the family are important. When we adults use precise words and terminology to discuss social interactions and respectfully resolve our own conflicts, we teach our children and teens to do these things in their own lives. When a parent demonstrates poise, confidence, and compassion in the face of tension or chaos, our children have a positive touchstone for their own appropriate social behavior.

You can teach your children about bullying outright, but veteran parents tell me the deepest, most transformative chats are those that take place casually and are revisited over time. For example, when watching a television show or reading a book featuring acts of interpersonal aggression, try asking your child to identify the type: relational aggression or verbal bullying? Look for opportunities to illustrate the difference between positive assertive and negative aggressive behaviors. Discuss positive ways of addressing and resolving conflicts.

Families will find it useful to keep a running discussion about the topic of healthy relationships in general. "We have regular conversations about how to make friends, be a friend, and what to value in friendships," said one parent in the survey. In these ongoing discussions about friendships and appropriate, healthy social interaction, parents can model the use of appropriate words in order to articulate emotions. As children near teens and adulthood, those discussions should broaden to include discussions about safe, mature, consensual romantic relationships. Clear language and healthy dialogue may help minimize the risk of sexual abuse and harassment.

Learning through Play

In addition to discussions, some children benefit from games or role-playing in order to puzzle through a bullying or other tense social situation. Several social-skills-oriented board games are available online, typically through businesses offering supplies to people who work with children on the autism spectrum or who have ADHD. Grok card games, for example, can be incorporated into weekly family game nights, giving all family members the opportunity to rehearse interpersonal skills in a supportive environment.

Budget-conscious families may have to shy away from investing in several games. Luckily, role-playing activities are free to all. Just like board games, role playing gives everyone a chance to rehearse socially appropriate actions and reactions to positive and negative social behaviors. It certainly does not hurt to try the activity a few times. Much like the classic party game Charades, participants can jot down social scenarios, toss them into a bowl, and then take turns drawing slips of paper to inspire improvised scenes. A little parental coaching may be called for in the beginning, but with practice, family members can experiment with confident physical postures and craft quick responses to verbal aggression. When addressing ordinary meanness and mild verbal bullying, light-hearted humor may be an appropriate response. For example, "Yes, thank you. I *am* weird," works for some kids who are targeted verbally for being outside the social norm. Other people prefer to rehearse saying firmly and unemotionally "Stop" or "Cut it out." Composure in delivery is critical.

When responding to a verbal bully, the real trick kids need to learn is to resist the urge to match the aggressor's level of meanness. Undercutting a bully's power requires stealth action to minimize escalation. This takes both skill and practice to master. When role-playing with older children, remind them how some verbal bullies can be derailed if the target displays surprisingly humane behavior, including compassion: "I liked your presentation today in class, but now you're being rude. Is something bothering you?" Some experts recommend the victim always use the aggressor's first name to remind the other child they are equals: "Gerald, you're out of line right now."

Previewing and Reviewing

Education and practice within the home is vital, as is the opportunity to try and hone skills out in public. A simple social skills teaching technique for the family to use when out is what I call "previewing and reviewing."[6] It is an elegant way to connect conversations to practice. Before attending a function, preview possible social pitfalls. Talk about what might happen and what might not happen, including how to react to sudden changes. These discussions should not be lectures but rather true, two-way conversations about what works in social settings. Review plans for managing conflict or emotional overwhelm if either occur. Afterward, review together what went right—and what went wrong—and discuss what could be done differently next time.

Over time, previewing and reviewing activities can become useful in helping manage expectations and correcting behavior. Of course, as a child matures and gains confidence, you can pull back on this practice.

Homeschoolers have an advantage when it comes to this sort of one-to-one nurturing. We parents can put up and take down the appropriate social and emotional learning scaffolds as we see fit, day in and day out. While there is an assumption in our culture that schools are the ideal environments for socialization, that is not always the case for some gifted/2e kids. At home with loving, thoughtful parents who offer a blend of support and challenge, children can develop social skills at a pace and to a degree that fits their makeup.

It is worth noting that each of the social skills development activities in this chapter can be modified for use in other learning communities, including homeschool cooperatives ("co-ops"), as we will discuss in the next chapter.

Chapter 6

Special Issues for Homeschool Families

As a [homeschool] parent, you don't have to settle for "good enough" and you don't have to jam your square peg into a round hole. You have the opportunity to construct a flexible, fluid solution that allows your child to flourish. ~Corin Barsily Goodwin and Mika Gustavson[1]

Because many families come to homeschooling due to a bullying event, it is tempting to think of homeschooling as a quiet refuge from bullying.

That is not always the case.

There is, obviously, the issue of bullying within families. Sadly, a small minority of homeschool families, just as in non-homeschool families, has engaged in hurtful interpersonal behaviors that have endangered the well-being of their children. These stories have made their way into news reports. Several of these cases were obviously domestic abuse situations. The children deserved closer scrutiny by law enforcement agencies and child protective services.

At the same time, children in healthy, loving, stable homeschool families can be exposed to bullying, too. This is largely because parents actively seek groups and classes to supplement their home curriculum or to provide kids with "socialization time" outside the home. Consequently, kids encounter bullying and relational aggression in homeschool co-ops, play groups, and innovative state-of-the-art microschool settings.

In contrast with their counterparts in traditional school settings, the parents of homeschool children who encounter bullies outside the home *must* work one-to-one with parents in resolving the problem. There is seldom an administrator to serve as a mediator. This undertaking requires strong interpersonal and conflict management skills. It may involve some tough choices with regard to one's social circle if a satisfactory resolution cannot be reached between families.

In the case of homeschool learning communities, parents' careful forethought can reduce the number of negative behaviors. Unfortunately, this sort of work is not something groups routinely do, but it is something we homeschool parents should insist upon for our children.

To that end, let us review a few strategies to help prevent bullying in a homeschool learning community or playgroup. As with the previous two chapters, feel free to take away from these suggestions what feels right for you and your family's situation.

First, Seek to Understand

Sooner or later the overwhelming majority of homeschool kids participate in one or more of the following types of groups: informal play groups, traditional after school programs, or formal private learning communities. When looking for a new educational opportunity for your family, it is vital that you pay close attention from the outset to how the groups are structured.

Open, nonhierarchical models of leadership are common in homeschool playgroups. This may sound ideal if you are inclined to relaxed structures, but these groups seldom have a clear plan in place for dealing with conflict. Participating families can have wildly different ideas about appropriate behavior, which can be a challenge for parents of 2e kids who are struggling to learn social norms. These children in particular require consistent messaging from adults and peers within their respective learning communities.

Furthermore, freewheeling playgroups frequently have a group of veteran parents who form the *de facto* leadership core. Whether or not these leaders are effective—or just another example of a playground-ruling clique—depends entirely upon the individual group.

Before joining any homeschool group—and especially if your child has had trouble with bullying in the past, ask upfront about processes and procedures for handling conflict. If you get the brush off from the group when you bring the topic up, then think carefully if such a group is worth it for the hour or two of activity it will provide. Might it create new problems? Can you give the group a trial run before committing? If you have a 2e kid who needs structure and support, then take a closer look at other socialization options first. This includes social skills classes offered by therapists and counselors. In other words, shop around before committing to a group or arrangement.

Many homeschoolers participate in traditional after school activities such as Boy Scouts and Girl Scouts. These organizations are more apt to be hierarchical in nature than homeschool co-ops and playgroups. In this case, the processes outlined in Chapter Four should work fine if a problem surfaces.

Lead When (and How) You Can

Over the last several years, I have hosted online workshops for new homeschool parents. Through this work I have watched several new homeschool parents of gifted/2e kids find themselves taking on another role after only a year or two of homeschooling, becoming educational entrepreneurs and signing on as a founding member of a co-op, microschool, or other independent learning community.

If you find yourself in this position, then you have a unique opportunity. Homeschoolers have a real need for parents who are unafraid to speak up about strategies to improve social relationships. If you are in the position of creating a new, formal learning community, propose to your group that time be designated to discuss bullying and how to prevent it. Depending upon the group, this could be a one-time unit study or a theme that is revisited at different times. Several national organizations now make available educational toolkits and curricula that address bullying, and these materials can be useful in traditional and non-traditional learning communities. PACER's National Bullying Prevention Center and StopBullying.gov are two excellent starting points (see Selected Resources).

When you bring up the topic of bullying, expect to encounter resistance. Many parents continue to believe it is *always* best to leave children to resolve their own conflicts. Indeed probably the lion's share of grown-ups fails to understand the subtle issues related to friendships and covert aggression. Gently remind your peers that positive social skills are as vital to success as history, language arts, or other subjects parents volunteer to oversee in a group setting. Isn't it time we, as a culture, started treating them as such?

You might try to impress upon others the value in assessing any special social needs within your homeschool learning community. This can be a critical first step in creating caring communities that support diverse learners. Once the information is collected (formally or informally), parents can look for ways to modify, if necessary, the learning community's written and unwritten rules.

If, for instance, a child in the group has a nut allergy, propose making the setting each week "nut free." Similarly, if some children have sensory needs, tailor the group schedule to allow all participants time to "get the wiggles out." Or permit the active kids to keep a different schedule, one that includes ample physical activity.

In accommodating and adapting for the diversity within the group, adult leaders will model acceptance and positive community building. They will also minimize the risk of vulnerable kids being targeted for bullying.

Remember, bullying can be symptomatic of a serious social flaw in any learning community. This can be rooted in a lack of proper oversight by parents at free time, poor group management skills, or interpersonal clashes between parents. Mean girls behavior happens between adults, too, and can play out between kids of "rival" families.

Hard Truths and High Hopes

As much as you may desire a co-op or other group education model to work, not every educational setting—no matter how ideal it sounds—works for every child. At the same time, a parent can want one thing and the kid another. Maybe you need regular one-on-one time with other adults but your kid needs to learn academics independently and is content to focus on maintaining a relationship with one special friend.

Rather than stewing in frustration at competing goals, experiment with different social schedules until you create an environment in which you and your child thrive. Host one or two children at a time in your backyard for a playdate with safe, quality snacks. Do not forget to incorporate positive socialization time for you with your own peers, as part of your personal self-care. Allow yourself to tweak and refine your routine and personal connections as necessary to create an optimal social experience.

Over time you will figure out what works—be it continuing with homeschooling or trying out another education model when your child is older. In the meantime, embrace the flexibility of homeschooling to create a warm, loving home and pleasant weekly routine that reflects everyone in your family's unique social development needs.

Epilogue

A few days before the first formal draft of this book was due to my publisher, my son and his closest friend, while enjoying a homeschool play date, encountered a bully in a local park. After trailing them around the play structures with minor verbal taunts, the other child yanked hard on my son's arm, twice. Within minutes I stood stunned as the boy's mother hurled expletives at me, threatening to physically beat me up for advising *both* of our kids—hers and mine, in a gesture of inclusiveness—to "Please keep your hands to yourself."

Rather than trying to match her rage, the three of us quietly walked away while the young woman ranted and raved. In the car on the way home, we reviewed the encounter. At first, we chuckled nervously at the false bravado displayed by the pair. Later we discussed how the duo deserved our compassion for the fact that, within their family, hostile actions are an accepted norm of interaction.

Reflecting upon the incident privately, I noticed how markedly different our reactions to the new bullying incident were from those we experienced in the wake of the homeschool park day incident. By nightfall the only thing left of the afternoon's bully encounter was a good story.

Together, we had learned to take our playground bullies in stride.

Selected Resources

Bullying (General)

Books

The Bully and the Bystander: From Preschool to High School—How Parents and Teachers Can Break the Cycle, by Barbara Coloroso

Bullied: What Every Parent, Teacher, and Kid Needs To Know About Ending the Cycle of Fear, by Carrie Goldman

Masterminds and Wingmen: Helping Our Boys Cope with Schoolyard Power, Locker-Room Tests, Girlfriends, and the New Rules of Boy World, by Rosalind Wiseman

Queen Bees and Wannabes: Helping Your Daughter Survive Cliques, Gossip, Boyfriends, and Other Realities of Adolescence, by Rosalind Wiseman

Queen Bee Moms and Kingpin Dads: Coping with the Parents, Teachers, Coaches, and Counselors Who Can Rule—or Ruin—Your Child's Life, Rosaline Wiseman, with Elizabeth Rapoport

Websites

It Gets Better Project
   http://www.itgetsbetter.org/
   With a mission to communicate to LGBTQ youth that life gets better, It Gets Better Project uses social media to educate, inform, and empower.

PACER's National Bullying Prevention Center
   http://www.PACER.org/Bullying
   A service of the Minnesota-based PACER Center serving families with disabilities, the website offers an expansive set of materials for students, parents, and educators. Of special interest are their Educator Toolkits and Activities: http://www.pacer.org/bullying/resources/toolkits/.

StopBullying.gov
> http://StopBullying.gov
> A project of the U.S. Department of Health and Human Services, this website also has a child- and teen-friendly site: StopBullying.gov/Kids/.

Gifted/2e Issues

Books

Dumbing Down America: The War on Our Nation's Brightest Young Minds (and What We Can Do to Fight Back), by James R. Delisle

Gifted Children: Myths and Realities, by Ellen Winner

Misdiagnosis and Dual Diagnoses of Gifted Children and Adults: ADHD, Bipolar, OCD, Asperger's, Depression, and Other Disorders, by James P. Webb, et al.

Ungifted: Intelligence Redefined, by Scott Barry Kaufman

Websites

Gifted Homeschoolers Forum
> http://giftedhomeschoolers.org/

Supporting the Emotional Needs of the Gifted
> http://sengifted.org/

Social Skills Development

Books

It's So Much Work to Be Your Friend: Helping the Child With Learning Disabilities Find Social Success, by Rick Lavoie

Trauma-Proofing Your Kids: A Parent's Guide to Instilling Confidence, Joy, and Resilience, by Peter A. Levine and Maggie Kline

The Unwritten Rules of Friendship: Simple Strategies to Help Your Child Make Friends, by Natalie Madorsky Elman and Eileen Kennedy-Moore

Websites

Grok Cards
> http://www.groktheworld.com/
> Rooted in non-violent communication principles, this website features several card-based activities to nurture social skills.

Social Thinking

http://www.socialthinking.com

> Founded by Michelle Garcia Winner, this website features books, posters, and other resources for teachers and parents, as well as information on upcoming training sessions held across the country.

Emotional Regulation, Psychology, and Mindfulness

Articles

"Grade-school bullying takes a toll on the adolescent brain, study finds," by Sarah D. Sparks, *Inside School Research*, November 17, 2014

"Inside the bullied brain: The alarming neuroscience of taunting," by Emily Anthes, *Boston.com*, November 28, 2010

"Mindfulness can literally change your brain," by Christina Congleton, Britta K. Hölzel, and Sara W. Lazar, *The Harvard Business Review*, January 8, 2015

Books

The Dialectical Behavior Therapy Skills Workbook: Practical DBT Exercises for Learning Mindfulness, Interpersonal Effectiveness, Emotion Regulation and Distress Tolerance, by Matthew McKay and Jeffrey C. Wood

Flow: The Psychology of Optimal Experience, by Mihaly Csikszentmihalyi

Parenting a Child Who Has Intense Emotions: Dialectical Behavior Therapy Skills to Help Your Child Regulate Emotional Outbursts and Aggressive Behavior, by Pat Harvey and Jeanine Penzo

Planting Seeds: Practicing Mindfulness with Children, by Thich Nhat Hahn

Teach, Breathe, Learn: Mindfulness In and Outside of the Classroom, by Meena Srinivasan

Understanding Myself: A Kid's Guide to Intense Emotions and Strong Feelings, by Mary C. Lamia

What to Do When Your Temper Flares: A Kid's Guide to Overcoming Problems with Anger, by Dawn Huebner

The author's other titles in this series deal with topics related to anxiety, worry, and fear, and all are excellent.

Websites

GoZen!

> http://www.GoZen.com
>
> GoZen! is a for-profit company that provides online programs and workbooks to help address childhood anxiety and worry while identifying and nurturing individual strengths.

Institute of Heart Math

> http://www.heartmath.org/
>
> This international non-profit is dedicated to helping reduce stress while building emotional resilience. Several books and other resources are available through the website.

Counseling

Gifted and Homeschool Friendly Professionals

> http://giftedhomeschoolers.org/resources/homeschooling/gifted-homeschool-friendly-professionals/
>
> This list of parent-recommended professionals throughout North America covers specialties such as assessment, counselors, education consultants, occupational and vision therapists, audiologists, and more.

Endnotes

Chapter 1

1. Medaris, Kim, "Study: Gifted children especially vulnerable to effects of bullying," *Purdue News Service*, (April 6, 2006), http://www.purdue.edu/uns/html4ever/2006/060406.Peterson.bullies.html.

2. Medaris, "Study."

3. Kaufman, Scott Barry, *Ungifted: Intelligence Redefined*, (New York: Basic Books, 2015), 92. (Referenced for an overview of the Columbus Group and its statement.)

4. Lereya, Suzet Tanya, William E. Copeland, E. Jane Costello, and Dieter Wolke, "Adult mental health consequences of peer bullying and maltreatment in childhood: two cohorts in two countries," *The Lancet Psychiatry* (April 28, 2015), www.thelancet.com/journals/lanpsy/article/PIIS2215-0366%2815%2900165-0/abstract.

5. Copeland, William E., Dieter Wolke, Suzet Tanya Lereya, Lilly Shanahan, Carol Worthman, and E. Jane Costello, "Childhood bullying involvement predicts low-grade systemic inflammation into adulthood," *Proceedings of the National Academy of Sciences of the United States* 111, no. 21 (May 12, 2014), 7570–7575, www.ncbi.nlm.nih.gov/pmc/articles/PMC4040559/.

6. Landau, Jennifer, *How to Beat Psychological Bullying*, (New York: The Rosen Group, 2013), 10. (Study cited.)

Chapter 2

1. Coloroso, Barbara, *The Bully and the Bystander: From Preschool to High School—How Parents and Teachers Can Break the Cycle*, (New York: William Morrow, 2009), 20.

2. Klein, George, *Elvis: My Best Man: Radio Days, Rock 'n' Roll Nights, and My Lifelong Friendship with Elvis*, (New York: Three Rivers Press, 2011), 17.

3. Klein, *Elvis*, x.

4. Merrill, Jen, *If This is a Gift, Then Why Can't I Send it Back? Surviving in the Land of Gifted and Twice-Exceptional*, (Olympia: GHF Press, 2012), 42.

5. Winner, Ellen, *Gifted Children: Myths and Realities*, (New York: Basic Books, 1997), 229.

6. Toldson, Ivory A., "The 'Acting White Theory' doesn't hold up," *The Root*, January 30, 2013, www.theroot.com/articles/politics/2013/01/acting_white_theory_black_academic_achievement_based_on_other_factors.html.

7. "Gifted Cubed," *Gifted Homeschoolers Forum*, last modified February 23, 2015, http://giftedhomeschoolers.org/ghf-press/gifted-cubed/.

8. Coloroso, *The Bully and the Bystander*, 167.

9. Coloroso, *The Bully and the Bystander*, 184.

Chapter 3

1. Coloroso, Barbara, *The Bully and the Bystander: From Preschool to High School—How Parents and Teachers Can Break the Cycle*, (New York: William Morrow, 2009), 75.

2. Kennedy-Moore, Eileen, "Is it bullying . . . or ordinary meanness?" *Psychology Today*, last modified September 30, 2014, https://www.psychologytoday.com/blog/growing-friendships/201409/is-it-bullyingor-ordinary-meanness.

3. Wallace, Kelly, "Brutally Honest: Mean Girls are Getting Younger," *CNN.com* video series, November 10, 2014, www.cnn.com/2014/11/10/living/brutally-honest-mean-girls-getting-younger/.

4. Credit to counselor Bob Yamtich for illuminating how minor aggressions can be instructive, if uncomfortable. Bob also taught me about Grok cards, mentioned as a resource later in the book.

5. Peplar, Debra J., Wendy M. Craig, and William L. Roberts, "Observations of aggressive and nonaggressive children on the school playground,"

Merrill-Palmer Quarterly, 1998, no. 44, 55-76, faculty.tru.ca/wlroberts/pepler,craig,roberts.pdf.

Chapter 4

1. Wiseman, Rosalind, "School bullying: what you haven't heard," *RosalindWiseman.com*, March 16, 2011, rosalindwiseman.com/going-back-to-the-basics-a-reality-check-on-bullying-prevention-tips/.

Chapter 5

1. Kashtan, Inbal, *Parenting From Your Heart: Sharing the Gifts of Compassion, Connection, and Choice*, (Encinitas: Puddledancer Press, 2014), 8.

2. Bowes, Lucy, Barbara Maughan, Avshalom Caspi, Terrie E. Moffitt, and Louise Arsenault, "Families promote emotional and behavioural resilience to bullying: evidence of environment effect," *The Journal of Child Psychology and Psychiatry* 51 (7), 809-817.

3. Levine, Peter A. and Maggie Kline, *Trauma-Proofing Your Kids: A Parent's Guide to Instilling Confidence, Joy, and Resilience*, (Berkeley: North Atlantic Books, 2008), 7.

4. Levine, *Trauma-Proofing Your Kids*, 7.

5. "Why do bullies bully?" *Mindful Magazine*, (February 2014), 24.

6. Lavoie, Richard, *It's So Much Work to Be Your Friend: Helping the Child With Learning Disabilities Find Social Success*, (New York: Touchstone, 2006). Note: As a parent, I began using the phrase "previewing and reviewing" at home well before I read Lavoie's book as part of my research. Lavoie mentions a similar approach ("previewing"), and his book is a good read for parents of kids with significant social challenges.

Chapter 6

1. Goodwin, Corin Barsily and Mika Gustavson, *Making the Choice: When Typical School Doesn't Fit Your Atypical Child* (Olympia: GHF Press, 2011), 49.

About the Author

Pamela Price is a GHF board member, gifted advocate, and writer based in San Antonio, Texas, where she lives with her husband and son. For several years prior to becoming a journalist, she worked as an academic and career advisor at The University of Texas at Austin.

Pamela may be reached via:

RedWhiteandGrew.com

Twitter (@RedWhiteandGrew)

Facebook (Facebook.com/RedWhiteandGrew)

Manufactured by Amazon.ca
Bolton, ON